LOVING
HER GOD'S
WAY

How a Man Can Love His Woman, and Please God

Loving Her God's Way: How a Man Can Love His Woman
and Please God
By Eric M. Watterson

CENTRY™ Curriculum
© 2022 All rights reserved.

ISBN: 979-8-371-50897-3

To access the online course attached to this book, and
others, visit us online at: CentryLeague.com

TABLE OF CONTENTS

Where There is Love There is Life.

~Mahatma Gandhi

THANK YOU

As a special thank you for purchasing this book, we offer you a FREE no obligation Manhood Mentoring or Quick Coach Audio Message to help you address any personal concerns you may have.

Sometimes we need another perspective on the situations and the circumstances we face in life. During these times, we're here to help.

For more information visit:
ManhoodMentor.me or QuickCoach.me

To Your Success,

Eric M. Watterson

Being deeply loved by someone gives you strength, while loving someone deeply gives you courage.

~ Lao Tzu

PART 1:

INTRODUCTION

"Complete my joy by being of the same mind, having the same love, being in full accord and of one mind."
~Philippians 2:2 ESV

A man that understands how to love and honor a woman does not see it as a job, but an honor. This book is meant to help and inspire those guys that want to be the types of men that our women and children need. While it is also meant to strongly oppose and fight against those mindsets and beliefs that destroy our relationships, marriages, families, communities and world.

Before we continue, I'd like to share a few upsetting statistics:
- On average, nearly 20 people per minute are physically abused by an intimate partner in the United States. During one year, this equates to more than 10 million women and men. [1]
- 1 in 4 women and 1 in 9 men experience severe intimate partner physical violence, intimate partner contact sexual violence, and/or intimate partner stalking with impacts such as

injury, fearfulness, post-traumatic stress disorder, use of victim services, contraction of sexually transmitted diseases, etc. [2]

- 1 in 3 women and 1 in 4 men have experienced some form of physical violence by an intimate partner. This includes a range of behaviors which may include slapping, shoving, pushing, etc." [3]

- On a typical day, there are more than 20,000 phone calls placed to domestic violence hotlines nationwide. [4]

- 1 in 5 women in the United States has been raped in their lifetime. [5]

Our Heavenly Father God wants His daughters and His children to experience love, honor and respect here on earth so that it's not completely foreign to them, when they get to heaven.

If the guys that say they love God here on Earth don't show women and children Gods kind of love, who will?

FROM THE HEART

"A loving heart is the truest wisdom."
~ Charles Dickens

I believe that when a man truly loves and honors a woman it benefits him in ways he'll never truly understand until he does it. When a man loves a woman with the type of love that wants to protect, cover and serve her, it benefits him because the more he gives love away, the more his heart opens up to receive and be filled with that same type of love in return. This type of perspective will make him stronger, and a quality man, as he purposely gives true love to his woman.

We understand that there are some guys that abuse, misuse, mistreat and dishonor women. We purposely stand apart and against them. As males that Serve, Honor & Protect, within the CENTRY Organization we highly value and esteem the essence of women. We place great value on the women we call our wives, on the mothers of our children, on the helpers of our lives, the carriers of the egg that receives our seed, and the "Female Ying" to our "Male Yang"! The purpose of this book is to illustrate the importance that we place upon women based on the love that God has for us all.

Our goal is to explain why we believe that males must stand united and properly serve, honor and protect women as the incubators of life and as gifts from the one true God, Our Heavenly Father. The honor of her must be more than a temporary mindset that males use to get what they want from women, it must become the standard that every quality male examines his life and actions by.

This is one reason why The CENTRY Brand exists. It's purpose is to assist, train and inspire males of every color, every creed and every background to stand up against the dishonor that our women and children have endured. We want to share this message with every male willing to listen.

Women are the source by which life enters the world. Every man ever born, came through the womb of a woman. Without women, there would be no men. So how much sense does it make for men to dishonor the source and avenue that was used to bring them life?

Women are a gift. They deserve to be loved, honored and cherished by men. It's time to show all women how much we love them and how much we honor them. If you disagree with us, this information is not for you. However, if you do agree, please join us in our mission and goal.

For True Sons

When we think of love, it's something that we hear so often that it's easy to underestimate and take for granted. 1 John 4:16 says, ***"God is love, and all who live in love live in God, and God lives in them." John 13:35 says, "By this everyone will know that you are my disciples, if you love one another."*** So, the act of love is not optional for those who claim to love God and are connected to Him through His Son, Jesus the Christ.

Now, if we take those two verses and combine their meaning, it's safe to say that, "**Because God is love,** this is especially **every child of God that has accepted Jesus Christ as their Lord and Savior, should display the same type of love for others that Jesus has displayed for us.**" So, displaying love and honor for women is not something that a True Son of God would choose to do on one day and then choose NOT to do on another.

Love is our lifestyle. It's who we are and what we do. Not to prove something to the people around us, but because we want to please our Father in Heaven and because He expects us to show love to others, because He has, through His Son, shown love to us.

So, "Loving Her God's Way" is not something that we expect the average dude to be strong enough to do. This is something for the True Sons of God. He expects it from us, and we will do everything we can, to please Him. That's just what sons do.

A Father's Reward

Imagine a wealthy and successful businessman that greatly loves his wife and family. He's well known for being fair, while also being generous to his employees, his neighbors and the poor. If this man gives generously to those he loves outside of his home, how much more will he give to his wife and children?

Now, imagine if he gives gifts to his kids, just for being his kids, how much more will he give to them when his kids love and honor their mother and his wife? When his kids help other people like he does? When his kids take ownership of the family business and want to walk in their father's shoes?

Matthew 7:11 NIV says, ***"If you, then, though you are evil, know how to give good gifts to your children, how much more will your Father in heaven give good gifts to those who ask him!"*** I personally believe that God is looking for ways to be a blessing to us and to reward us. When we get to Heaven, I believe we'll be rewarded by God for the simple acts of love we've shown, like saying "Good morning!", to a stranger or letting someone cut in front of us during rush hour traffic.

So, if God wants to reward us, as Sons of God, for the simple things we do, how much more will He reward us for loving His daughters that He has entrusted into our hands? How much more will He reward us for His Little Children that He entrusted to us to help raise as parents, leaders and authority figures that point them towards the purpose for their lives?

Why? Because He created and owns everything that is and He's looking for ways to share what He has with us. He wants to reward every guy that loves others and treats them well. It's as simple as that! I believe this is especially true for women and children, because they are created weaker, in terms of physical strength than the average guy. So, abusing and mistreating them can be easy for any dude that's weak minded and selfish.

I was at a school one day and a grade schoolboy pushed a little girl down. I asked him why he did that, and he responded with, "Because I can." Of course, I wanted to smack the taste out of his mouth! However, I just shook my head knowing that his acts are being recorded and will be returned upon him or his family one day unless he changes his ways and allows God's grace to step in and maybe adjust some of the ways he's living his life, even as a young boy.

So, as you read through this material, never forget that there's a God in Heaven that is looking for ways to reward those that express His love here on earth. How much of a reward do you want?

Question

Do you see yourself as a Son of God? If so, do you "really believe" you can live and love like Your Heavenly Father does?

WHAT'S HAPPENING?

"He who wants to do good, knocks at the gate; he who loves finds the gates open." ~R. Tagore Thakur

A true story… *"Not long ago, I got up early to head to the gym and saw a car stranded just outside a gas station near the street. I looked closely to see a young pregnant woman standing near it, so I turned around and asked her if she was ok. She immediately thanked me for stopping, told me she had run out of gas and asked if I would help. Her car was too large to push up to the pump by myself. It was one of those big, long cars made of steel! Kinda like that 1974 Dodge Monaco that the Blues Brothers drove. Basically, a tank on wheels! Anyway, I purchased a gas can, put a few dollars in it and put the gas in her car.*

While helping her, she proceeded to tell me that I was the fourth guy to stop, but the only one that didn't ask for some type of sexual favor in return for my help. Shocked by her statement, I continued to pour gas in her tank. Once her vehicle had started, she still expected me to make some type of sexual request from her for my help. She was so persistent in it that I had to literally drive off and leave her there. As I drove away, I could see her standing there watching me from my rear-view mirror. I think she expected me to turn around and come back."

Why would this happen? Why would a woman in need be shocked that a guy would help her and require nothing in return but hopefully a smile and thank you? Why would any woman expect to have to perform a sexual act in return for a man's assistance?

It would probably be safe to say that the majority of the men that this woman had encountered before meeting me, would have taken from her before giving to her. This is a serious problem!!! Childish males are destroying the God-given support and gifts that we have in our wives, mothers, daughters and sisters at an alarming rate. Of course, there're good men out there that are exceptions to this rule. However, these exceptions are too few and need to increase drastically! It's important that we teach quality standards to our youth and other guys, so that the "exceptions" don't experience "extinction".

Question

Have you done something for a woman, from the kindness of your heart, and she "expected" you to want something in return?

MEDIA INFLUENCE

"Do not judge your neighbor until you walk two moons in his moccasins." ~Cheyenne

The saying, "You are what you eat." also applies to what you "eat" spiritually. Advertisements, TV, movies, music, music videos, news, social media, etc., are all avenues by which you "eat." What you are "eating" or exposing yourself to creates ideas, images, concepts and thoughts that will affect your mind, your thinking and your life.

The influence of the media can change the minds of the masses simply by repeating the same message over and over, whether or not the message is true or not. For example, a message through music that expresses having several sexual partners as acceptable and cool displays a message that says using women as objects without commitment or marriage is normal. There are songs and artists that label women with derogatory terms, elevate casual sex and display disrespect for authority while also diminishing the expression of kindness and love. It's these types of messages that when received over and over will take root in the minds of guys and negatively affect their relationships and how they interact with women and others.

Years ago, TV shows would show a married couple sleeping in separate beds. Now you have couples of all kinds, in all kinds of positions sleeping in the same bed, married or not, on the big, little and tiny screens. So, if a concept is seen and expressed over and over, eventually what was wrong years ago will be deemed "right," not because the actual concept has become "right," but because it's been shared so much that we begin to "accept it" as right. It was wrong to abuse a woman 60 years ago, and it's still wrong today, no matter how many social media posts, songs, videos, movies or TV shows say it's ok.

Quality males decide to do what's beneficial for others and resist those things that are destructive and selfish. We must not allow the deceptive and distorted messages of the media to plant thoughts and concepts within us that keep us from being the quality men, brothers, husbands and fathers that our women and children need.

Question

What types of media do you eat and what kinds of thoughts are being created within you?

THE PROCESS OF DEVELOPMENT

Anger repressed can poison a relationship as surely as the cruelest words. ~Dr. Joyce Brothers

Think about the process of development from infancy to adulthood. What we hear, what we're exposed to and what we're taught becomes the foundation of who and what we become in life.

One day I watched a documentary about a racist organization on the History Channel. During the program, they showed a photograph of a small child wearing a white hood, surrounded by taller adults wearing hoods as well. If that was the way this child was raised, trained and taught, can we really blame them if they grow up to live a lifestyle of division and hatred?

Of course, we don't agree with this type of lifestyle or belief system. The United States Constitution states that, *"We hold these truths to be self-evident, that all men are created equal, that they are endowed by their Creator with certain unalienable Rights that among these are Life, Liberty and the pursuit of Happiness."* However, if this type of destructive mindset was instilled in a person as a child, when they grow up, it becomes a part of "who" they are, because of "what" they have been raised to believe and accept during their process of development despite what the laws of our great land teach and are founded on.

The average toys for little girls are doll houses, baby dolls and toy kitchens. While the toys for boys, at the same age, are bouncing balls, water guns, action figures and play swords. Little girls are given toys that expose them to caring for a house and kids, preparing fake eggs and having tea parties.

On the other hand, little boys are given toys that bounce, guns that shoot, action figures that fight and cars that race. While little girls are being trained for adult responsibilities and family life, little boys are being trained for adult fun and bigger toys.

Women are trained from a young age to accept and learn responsibility. They see it as fun and look forward to becoming a Barbie wife to the perfect Ken husband that always comes home after work. On the opposite end, and at the same time, men are trained to compete, be better than the next guy, play ball, destroy whatever they can get their hands on, pile their broken toys in the corner and ask for new ones. So, do girls really develop or mature faster than boys, or are we allowing our boys to play while teaching our girls to be responsible?

Studies have shown that a child develops the key skills that determine who they become as adults, during the early years of life. So, if boys are trained to play, it will take a lot of work to teach them responsibility when he becomes a man. It doesn't just happen when he meets a good woman.

Know it or not, a boy learns to be a man from a man. Unfortunately, little boys are learning to be big boys from older boys, which continues the cycle of playing among males. We need to be honest about the immaturity in males and make sure that we understand that the process of development is not automatic.

Boys must be trained to be men by quality and mature men, if our women are ever to be loved, honored and treated the way they need and deserve to be treated.

Question

Do the majority of the guys you have around you honor or dishonor women?

Do you think they effect how you treat women?

When you think about your personal process of development, were you trained from a boy to become a quality husband and father? If so, how?

THE LOSS OF STANDARDS

"Money cannot buy peace of mind. It cannot heal ruptured relationships, or build meaning into a life that has none." ~Richard M. DeVos

Another true story... *"Not long ago, I was in a Kinko's getting something printed. A young lady at the paper cutter dropped a bunch of her cards on the floor. I immediately got out of line and said, "I've got it," and proceeded to pick up all the cards off the floor. After I was done, she thanked me and I continued to wait to be served. A few moments later, an older gentleman said to me, "Where are you from?" "Philly," I replied. "Really? I didn't think they taught those types of manners there. Ya don't see many young men being kind anymore." he said to me.*

Why would this happen to me? How many other kind men are surprising to the people that see them? There used to be a standard of quality that males were judged by. These standards showed our women that they deserved to be respected and honored. There should be a standard that tells a man to never hit a woman but always honor her. A standard that explains to young boys that girls are made physically weaker, so treat them as such and don't abuse them. There should be standards

27

in our society that men operate by to help women feel appreciated and loved.

Without quality standards in place, males have nothing to measure themselves against. Standards help set a mark and a level of accountability for our actions. Without a standard that displays honor for women, guys will continue to mistreat and dishonor them because there is no standard in place to judge themselves by when they don't. Without established standards and beliefs that we use to judge our lives by, there's nothing to hold us accountable for our actions.

In our society, we've allowed some of our vitals standards and areas of personal accountability to be removed. Without quality standards and beliefs to govern ourselves by, there's nothing to keep us from acting on whatever selfish or evil thought that comes to mind. If you are to become a male of quality, there must be a set of quality standards that you live by that govern the way you treat and honor women.

Question

If a man's standards determine how he treats a woman, what types of standards does every man need to live by?

THE UNDER
APPRECIATION OF WOMEN

"It takes two to tangle."
~ Unknown

Women are amazing. They're attractive, versatile, strong, intelligent, naturally giving and sincerely caring. Why else did God choose them to give birth? If the average guy had to push out another human being from between his legs, he'd probably rather be shot or dropped off a cliff. So, women deserve all the respect in the world for what they endure for the sake of their husbands, families and the furtherance of the human race.

As men, we sometimes ignore the importance of our women and take them for granted. A woman has the kids, a woman turns a house into a home and a woman can propel a man into success with her encouragement and support. All of which, some men seem to ignore or are just too selfish to recognize. In addition to what women do to please men, they deal with the constant challenges that come with just being a woman. Women wear makeup, style their hair and wear heels! And let's not mention the monthly cycle thing! Women do so much to be pleasing to us physically, and it shows. We men don't understand how they do it, but we love to see it!

Men love the end result, yet most of the time, we have no idea how much work, time and effort is needed to maintain it. Also, the God-given shape of a woman is something to be admired, not solely used for pleasure. And what about that wife that some husbands have that keep their bodies fit and together! It's a gift from God that just can't be described.

In essence, we men need to open our eyes and hearts to see all that women do to support, help and be pleasing to us. We need to recognize that the reason we take them for granted is because of another issue that we deal with…selfishness. A male who doesn't have the capacity to see the value of a woman may quite frankly be too immature, distracted, ignorant, childish, selfish or was never taught to see it. This is something we need to fix.

Question

Are men in our society increasing, or decreasing, in their love and respect for women, children, authority figures and others?

THE SELFISHNESS OF MEN

"Love is when the other person's happiness is more important than your own." ~H. Jackson Brown, Jr.

Little boys, no matter what their age, have a limited and childish perspective on life, called selfishness. Selfish little boys think about themselves, what they need and what they want with very little regard for others. They easily pass blame and make judgments based solely on what they want, what they need and how others have failed them. Some men have done this a lot when it comes to the love and care they show women.

A selfish man feels he should be served, instead of being willing to serve. A selfish and childish man would feel that his wife should automatically submit, instead of creating an atmosphere of love and honor where she would want to submit. A selfish and childish man expects to lead, instead of creating the conditions that make it easy for his woman to follow.

Now we aren't purposely coming down on men. We believe in properly teaching males what it means to be quality men. We are not joining the side of men bashing but the side of men training.

And to be honest, we know that women definitely have their part to play.

However, we believe that the rise and fall of a sound relationship is rooted in a guys ability to give his woman the love and honor she needs so that their relationship will continually grow and prosper. Another thing that some guys seem to ignore or just don't understand is the process where you first "Give" and then you "Take". Or the process of "Seed > Time > Harvest." When we first "give" to a woman, we "then" create a position for us to "receive" from her what we gave her in return.

So guys, please don't just take, take and then take some more, and then wonder why your woman becomes empty and has nothing left to give you. You took it all and didn't give anything back. Learn to sow a "seed", and give it time to grow and then you will reap a "harvest" from what you have sown.

If you see a woman who already has a plush garden and you just use the fruits in her garden until its bare, without doing any planting of seeds yourself, her garden will eventually run dry. This is a process that God has set up to create strong and lasting relationships between a man and his woman. We will discuss this again a little later.

Question

In your opinion, what's the main focus of the messages in movies, music, videos, social media, etc. concerning women mostly about, love or lust?

Do these messages make the guys more selfish in the way they love, honor and treat women?

To love and be loved is to feel the sun from both sides.

~ David Viscott

PART 2:

SUBMISSION

Submit yourselves therefore to God. Resist the devil, and he will flee from you. ~James 4:7 ESV

We submit to waiters and cooks when we go out to eat. We submit to doctors and dentist when we get health checkups and physicals. We submit to teachers and professors to help us learn and understand. We submit to parents and authority figures for protection and guidance.

Submission, in the proper context, is not just expected but it's often very good and is much more beneficial to us than we realize. From my experience as a teacher, the schools that seem to have the highest behavioral issues are those where the students don't understand how to submit to their teachers or understand how it benefits them when they do.

Submission is a way of life. So, in the proper context, is it really a bad thing?

THE GOD OPTION

"This day I call the heavens and the earth as witnesses against you that I have set before you life and death, blessings and curses. Now choose life, so that you and your children may live." ~Deuteronomy 30:19

Have you ever wondered about what makes God so powerful, strong, lovable and the one in true and ultimate control? I have and one conclusion that always comes to mind when I try and make sense in my limited thinking, is that He is God, unchangeable and unmoved whether we believe in Him or not, whether we follow Him or not and whether we obey Him or not.

One of the most powerful things that makes God, God to me is that He has made Himself optional in our lives. Revelation 3:20 NIV says, ***Here I am! I stand at the door and knock. If anyone hears my voice and opens the door, I will come in and eat with that person, and they with me.*** God has made Himself optional in our lives and has setup unimaginable rewards for those who choose Him. He is not making us choose Him. He wants to be chosen and has given us the right to choose or deny Him. How powerful is that?!

You know the one thing that I believe Heaven will be full of? People that chose to be there. There may be some people that chose God when they were young after going to church with grandma and never attended church again, some that chose to receive Jesus Christ on their death bed and some who chose Him in private and lived their lives trying to be the best Christian they could be. But regardless, I personally believe that everyone will remember when they chose God.

God is so powerful that He has made Himself and His Kingdom optional. Only those He draws to the love and sacrifice of His Son Jesus Christ will experience the fullness of what He has for them.

So, when it comes to how God wants us to treat and love His daughters, it's a choice. A guy can choose to love and honor her in a way that'll please her Heavenly Father, or he can abuse and mistreat her with little to no regard of her Heavenly Father that's looking down and taking note. It's all optional; at least right now it is.

1 Corinthians 3:13 NIV says, ***"their work will be shown for what it is, because the Day will bring it to light. It will be revealed with fire, and the fire will test the quality of each person's work."***

As we continue, we'll be discussing perspectives and thoughts that are optional for how a guy treats a woman. However, there will never be a sacrifice or an act of love that you do from your heart for your woman, child or others that's intended to bring glory and honor to God and His Kingdom, that He will not reward you for.

And you can take that to the bank!

Question

God has made himself "optional" in our lives because He wants to be chosen; and because He wants to reward us for choosing Him.

So, what will you choose?

WHEN GUYS SUBMIT

"Submit yourselves therefore to God. Resist the devil, and he will flee from you." ~James 4:7 ESV

Submission is a word that women sometimes find hard to accept because they don't want to be controlled. This actually makes a lot of sense because there are many selfish and childish guys that use the term "submission" the wrong way, in an attempt to control women.

The word submission is something that a lot of people think is just for wives in marriage. However, I actually feel that it's much more important for the husbands than it is for the wives. The word "submit" means: *"to give over or yield to the power or authority of another, to yield oneself to the power or authority of another, and/or to allow oneself to be subjected to some kind of treatment"*.

Let's remove the negative connotations that come with the word "submission" and let's talk in a general sense. First, let's replace the word 'submission' with another word of similar meaning like: "surrender, comply or yield". All have the same general meaning as the word submission. Instead of discussing submission in a marriage relationship lets discuss it from a working relationship. If your boss, the head of a company, makes a decision for the company, your job as an employee, would be to submit, or yield, to him or her. Why? Because he or she should have desires or goals that would make submitting or yielding to them not only right, but easy.

For example, if your boss wants your company to succeed, their decisions are meant to benefit the company. Your boss's main concern should be the mission, the growth and the expansion of the company. With that said, following their lead should be easy because when the company succeeds, you continue to get paid. Anyone that cannot follow or submit to that type of boss, most likely has an issue with authority, and the actual act of submission is not the problem.

Now let's apply the same conditions to a marriage relationship. (Please note that we're stressing submission in a "marriage" here. Without a marriage, where God the Father is the head, submission for a woman may not be correct. We strongly suggest that women only submit to men that are submitted to God. If a woman submits to, or even dates, a man that's not submitted to God, she is, by her own choice, submitting to whatever that male may be submitting to, which might be evil, lust, destruction or just the devil!).

A man should see his marriage as an organized covenant made before God where he knows he is accountable to abide within God's standards and principles on how he leads his family and treats the woman that God has allowed to become his wife. In this case, the wife is supporting, or "submitting" to the "mission" of the husband to love and lead his house properly. Something he cannot do successfully without her. Actually, without the husband and the wife, there's no covenant, no relationship, and no marriage that needs a mission. The two are equally important.

A man should lead others, and especially his woman in a way that continues to move their relationship toward success. He should also make decisions for the good of the relationship, and not just for himself. Unfortunately, there are many married men that quite frankly aren't good leaders and expect their wife to serve them when, in fact, as the head, it's his job to serve her first. When a woman knows "the heart" of her husband and that he truly loves her enough to make decisions that he feels are best for them as a whole, she will find ease in submitting to him, and be in a better position to help him. In this case she will find it easier to submit to his mission which should be the success of their relationship and marriage.

In essence, we believe that a man that truly loves and serves his wife won't have a problem getting her to submit or receive his love. We believe that Gods desire is not for women to just blindly submit to men; His desire is for women to submit to His love directly from Him and through men that are already submitted to Him. The problem is that some men aren't truly submitted to God's love and then they expect women to submit to them.

Men, ask yourself this, "Have I laid down my needs, my desires, my goals and my life for my woman, like Christ did for me?" Instead of trying to force or require submission, become a man that's submitted to God's love first and let her submit to the love of God that she receives from you as God's son.

Question

Before reading this, what did you think about the term "submission" in reference to marriage? What do you think about it now?

AS CHRIST LOVES

[25] For husbands, this means love your wives, just as Christ loved the church. He gave up his life for her [26] to make her holy and clean, washed by the cleansing of God's word. [27] He did this to present her to himself as a glorious church without a spot or wrinkle or any other blemish. Instead, she will be holy and without fault. [28] In the same way, husbands ought to love their wives as they love their own bodies. For a man who loves his wife actually shows love for himself. [29] No one hates his own body but feeds and cares for it, just as Christ cares for the church. ~Ephesians 5:25-29

This is one of the best scriptures I think husbands should use to learn how to love their wives. Not just based on the implications of what will happen when they do, but also because it directly compares husbands, or men, to Jesus. Looking and acting like Jesus is something that the "<u>True Sons of God</u>" pursue.

These are guys that are committed to doing the best they can, to resemble our Lord and Savior Jesus Christ. 1 John 4:15 says, "***<u>Whoever confesses that Jesus is the Son of God, God abides in him, and he in God.</u>***" So, this scripture gives guys a unique opportunity to Love Like Jesus Christ!

Let's not rush pass that statement. We have been given the ability to "Love Like Christ". Now if we have the ability to "Love Like Christ" and God loves us like He loves Christ, then God will reward us as He has rewarded and is still rewarding Christ. Are you getting this?

We have an opportunity to receive rewards from God for loving the women and wives in our lives the same way Christ loves the Church and gave himself for it. This is one of the reasons why I believe the enemy fights guys in showing love and honor to women. Because "that fool, the devil" knows how Great a Reward God will give guys that show love and honor to His daughters that he entrusts into their hands!

Are you listening fellas?! This isn't a small thing! This is huge! Scripture compares showing love to a woman, to Christ dying on the cross! At face value, it's not a fair comparison. Your blood and my blood lacked the spiritual power to redeem us and pay the debt of sin, so only Jesus could do that. *(This is why He's Really The Only Way! For Real Real! But we won't go there right now. That's a topic for another time!)* But God in His Grace is willing to reward men in a similar way He rewarded Christ!

I don't know about you, but the possibility of doing something that would please God as much as Jesus pleases God is enough for me to be all in!

I will admit that I don't fully understand "why" He would reward us like Christ for loving women, but I do have my theories. There's a lot of things I don't understand about the Creator of Heaven and Earth. So I'm jumping all in by faith expecting to understand it better as I go! So, lets briefly discuss Ephesians 5:25-29, verse by verse, to see if we can break this down a little more and see how greatly God wants to reward us for walking in love.

Ephesians 5:25

"For husbands, this means love your wives, just as Christ loved the church. He gave up his life for her."

In this verse, I'd like to focus on how love and sacrifice are connected. Jesus Christ "**loved**" and because He loved He "**gave**". And not just gave but gave His life for the church. I think one of the main things that we guys need to realize is that when we lay down our lives for our wives, we act in love towards them, in the same way that Christ acted in love towards us.

However, the part that I think is missed or overlooked here, is that Christ laid down His life as a seed and received a countless harvest of souls that are committed to Him and the Kingdom of God because of what He did. He laid down His life, and received in return, the multitude of lives that love Him and are committed to Him and the Kingdom of God.

So as husbands, when we sacrifice ourselves for the benefit of our wives, we set ourselves up to receive an abundant harvest as a result. Christ will eternally be rewarded for laying down His life for us. What kind of eternal reward will you receive when you love your wife with the same type of intense selfless love that Christ loved you with?

<u>Ephesians 5:26</u>
"<u>...to make her holy and clean, washed by the cleansing of God's word.</u>"

Jesus spoke over and over about how He only did what He saw His Father do. Jesus used God's Word to help Him fulfill the mission before Him and to cover and cleanse us by speaking life and love over us. In John 8:11, He told the woman caught in the act of adultery, ***"<u>Go now and leave your life of sin.</u>"***

He did not speak over her words of death or even accusation. But instead spoke life over her and told her she could do something that she may never have thought was possible on her own. He told her to *"...leave your life of sin."* I wonder if she would have ever considered it being possible to leave her life of sin if Jesus would have never spoken it over her.

As men, we have the opportunity to cover women in ways that will build them up and make them feel strong and confident within themselves by using words that make them feel loved, valuable, beautiful and wanted. Women that don't get these simple words of love from fathers, brothers and husbands may look for other ways to feel valuable and significant. I think this is one of the reason Instagram and social media seems so fulfilling to females because it gives them a platform to have someone affirm them in ways they may never have received from a father or a husband.

As a Man of God, you should use your words to wash over and build up the women in your life. This would include not only your wife, but also your daughters, stepdaughters, nieces, sisters, cousins, etc., with words that create thoughts that will help them to know that they're valuable and loved by you and their Father in Heaven.

Ephesians 5:27

"He did this to present her to himself as a glorious church without a spot or wrinkle or any other blemish. Instead, she will be holy and without fault."

Scripture indicates that Jesus did what He did to help us become what we couldn't be without Him. He did what He did to present us to Himself as a Glorious church without spot or wrinkle. Now, I don't know about you, but I've got a lot of spots and wrinkles in my life. However, because I'm in Jesus, I have the opportunity to be as glorious as He is. He did what He did for me, to make me a better son for Him and The Father's Kingdom.

When a man loves and honors his woman, he's helping her to become something she wasn't before he was in her life. He's on purpose sowing love and honor into her, that helps her to shine and glow as a woman loved and honored by her man. There's never a kind word, loving act or act of service that you sow into your woman that doesn't benefit you.

Ephesians 5:28

"In the same way, husbands ought to love their wives as they love their own bodies. For a man who loves his wife actually shows love for himself."

When a man loves his wife, he's really loving himself. Now to understand this better I think it's important that we remember that from God's standpoint, He sees beyond just the physical body to the spiritual body and the essence He created it to be.

For example, male and female fit together through their sexual organs, or members. When the male penis is inserted into the female vagina, the two different sexual members create a connection that is unique in itself.

In the same way, when the spiritual essence of a male is joined with the spiritual essence of a female, the combining of these two separate spirits creates a new unique spiritual combination that doesn't exist anywhere else in creation. This is why sex is so important to God, because when a man and female join, they recreate the essence of the very first being He created in the Garden of

Eden, Adam. It's the two separate and opposite beings and spirits that creates a new flesh.

So, when a man, abuses or dishonors his wife, he's actually hurting himself because in the Spirit Realm, he and his wife are one. If a man purposely hurts his wife, he's performing an act of Spiritual "Self-Injury" or "Self-Harm".

Self-injury can be categorized as an act of rebellion and/or rejection of their parents' values and a way of individualizing oneself. Sufferers may feel that self-injury is a way of expressing self-hatred; for punishing themselves for strong feelings or for being bad and undeserving in some way that deserves abuse. [6]

With this in mind, when a man abuses a woman, he is abusing himself. The question then becomes, "Does he know he's hurting himself and does he feel like he deserves to be hurt which is why he's hurting the woman close to him?"

Ephesians 5:29
"No one hates his own body but feeds and cares for it, just as Christ cares for the church."

This scripture makes it clear that when a man loves and honors his woman, he is loving and honoring himself. The other side of this statement implies that when a man hurts, disrespects and abuses his wife, he is in essence hurting, disrespecting and abusing himself.

Christ cares for the church past, present and future. He is ever interceding for us even now. The nail marks in His hands, from His sacrifice for us on the cross, is a constant reminder to all of Heaven, that the price for sin has been paid and that the Gift of Right Standing in the Kingdom of God is available for anyone who will receive Jesus Christ as their Lord and Savior.

God has given every man on this planet the opportunity to be rewarded for showing love and honor to the woman that come across his path. But the devil is actively fighting against this plan.

If we really want to be expressions of what Jesus did for us, it's imperative that we show love, honor and respect for the women God places in our lives, It's our privilege and honor to cover them, to love them and to serve them just as Jesus Christ does for us!

Question

What kind of reward do you want to receive for the love and honor you gave to the women and children that were in your life?

If you want a good reward tomorrow, you should treat them with love and honor today.

GOD'S PURPOSES

"Many are the plans in the mind of a man, but it is the purpose of the Lord that will stand."
~Proverbs 19:21 ESV

When we think about the attractiveness of women. How they draw us guys to them with their walk, their voice, their kindness and their shapes. It's kind of amazing sometimes to be honest. Do you ever just find yourself saying, "Wow God!" "Why did You do that? Why did you make her so fine, or her so crazy?" Ok, just kidding…a little.

But seriously, what are the purposes of God? I'm not saying I know for sure, because that would simply be unwise. But I believe He will reveal somethings to those that truly want to walk in His ways as a Son of The Kingdom. So, let's briefly talk about some of the purposes I believe our loving Father has put in place for our lives with our women here on Earth.

For Creation

Imagine that 3 separate planes crash on 3 separate, and secluded, tropical islands in the middle of the ocean. The first plane crashes on "Island A" with 2 Women on board; the second plane crashes on

53

"Island B" with 2 Men onboard, and; the third plane crashes on "Island C" with 1 Woman and 1 Man onboard. Each plane is untraceable and isn't found for 30 years.

What do you think they will find on each island? Let's just imagine:

- "Island A" there's two women braiding each other's hair and collecting seashells.
- "Island B" there's two men building tree houses and playing soccer with coconuts.
- "Island C" either the male or the female is cooking, while the other one is in the sea fishing as a bunch of kids run around on the beach laughing and playing.

Every legal and verified human being walking on the planet has come through the womb of a woman. It's the combination of egg and sperm that keeps life going on the planet.

This is God's purpose and plan. And it's good. Really Good!

For Order

If you've never seen the movie "The Shack" I highly recommend it as a great Christian movie with a strong message of forgiveness and faith.

One of the greatest concepts among many that the movie expressed was the image of the Trinity in the person of God the Father, God the Son and God the Spirit. And while expressing the concept the human character interacting with God questioned who's in charge. God responded with something like we are one, there's no competition between them.

I love that message because it expresses that yes there is an order to the God head, but there's love and acceptance within that order. While God has created the family structure, there's not one that's greater or lesser I believe. There just must be order because anything with two heads is a monster. And a car with two steering wheels will never make it out of the driveway.

God is a God of order. As men, it's important that we understand and respect that order not to say we are any greater than any women or child, but because God has put order in place so that's it's easier to discuss a direction and hold someone accountable for the entire unit reaching its destination. Men are no greater than the women and children God wants them to cover and lead. If anything, he may be the lesser one because his actions will be more greatly weighed when it comes to how he has loved and covered those God gifted to his charge.

For Relationships

Genesis 2:18 NIV says, ***"The LORD God also said, "it is not good for the man to be alone. I will make a helper suitable for him.***" I believe that God is a God of relationships. He has a quality relationship with His Son and Spirit, and He wants us to have quality relationships as well.

There's nothing like the feeling that a guy gets when his woman loves and supports him. While there's also no other feeling that can be as destructive and hurtful like when the woman he loves, undermines and disrespects him, especially in public or in front of others. God wants the relationships that His sons and daughters have, to grow and flourish here on Earth and ultimately continue into Heaven and beyond.

So, make the most of every relationship you have. Make sure to put them where they belong in your heart and don't purposely burn bridges with dishonor or disrespect.

For Rewards

As we discussed before, God is looking ways to reward you. Hebrews 13:2 NIV says, **_"Do not forget to show hospitality to strangers, for by so doing some people have shown hospitality to angels without knowing it."_** This is just another way that what we do in life is being recorded so God can show us love and reward us in the next life for all the love we have shown to others.

I believe God wants to see who will truly take on His nature and show love to the people around them, despite how people treat you. It's God's will to reward us for walking in love and being a light in a dark world. Don't miss out on your reward. If you don't want it, send it to me!

For Jesus the Christ

Hebrews 12:2 NIV says, **_"...For the joy set before him he endured the cross, scorning the shame, and sat down at the right hand of the throne of God."_** There's a Heavenly reward that we never fully understand that Jesus endured for us. And when we partner with Him in His mission to reunite man with the purposes of God, we partner with Him and carry our own cross for God's Kingdom.

I don't know about you, but day after day, I wanna try and become more like my Lord and Savior so that when I stand before The Father, I hear Him say well done. As men of God one of the best ways to please Him is to see every person as an expression of His love and someone that Jesus Christ laid down His life so that they can have all that The Kingdom of God has to offer.

When we value the women, the children and the relationships we have, we show God that we value Him and all that our Lord and Savior Jesus Christ has done for us.

Question

Do you believe that God has a purpose for you and for the relationship with you and every woman you meet?

If so, always seek to understand God's purpose and His Grace will follow.

EMBRACING GRACE

"But he gives more grace. Therefore it says, "God opposes the proud, but gives grace to the humble."
~James 4:6 ESV

So, let's be honest, saying we're gonna love our women, our children, our family members and random strangers unconditionally is much easier said than done. Most of us have intentions of being the best Christians in the World while sitting in church, listening to a message or watching a Christian video on YouTube. It's when we are away from church, sitting in traffic or dealing with negative feelings and emotions that we really need to apply the standards and principles that express God's Kingdom. However, God knows that we are human, and we need help doing that.

To help us, He's provided us with His Grace through Jesus Christ so we can love with His strength, not our own. It's up to us to connect with that Grace by faith, and use it, to conquer and to win, in our everyday lives.

The Grace Position

When we think of God's Grace there seems to be a simple and powerful understanding that most

59

seem to accept based on Romans 3:24 (ESV) which says, *"...and are justified by his grace as a gift, through the redemption that is in Christ Jesus,"* and Romans 5:15 (ESV) which says, *"...but the free gift is not like the trespass. For if many died through one man's trespass, much more have the grace of God and the free gift by the grace of that one man Jesus Christ abounded for many."*

There are several different viewpoints and types of grace explained within the Body of Christ that many great books have been written to discuss and expound upon, so we won't focus too much on that here.

However, for our purposes here of learning how to love and honor our women and wives in a way that pleases God, I want us to focus on Grace as, **"God's power and ability given to us through the finished works of Jesus to help us do, what we could not do, on our own."**

So, our Grace Position is quite simply a stance that says, *"I can't do it on my own God. I need Your Help, and Your Grace, to win and be successful in every area of life. Including how I love and honor my wife, my children, my family and others.*

As a human being, I don't have it in myself to show Your Love to others, so please give me Your Grace to love the people around me so that they experience Your Love through me, in Jesus Name."

So, with that said, the next few topics of Grace will be from the perspective of God's Grace flowing through our lives and out to the world around us.

Grace To Be Different

As we've already discussed, when we consider the typical mindset that the men in our society have, we see a negative mindset and treatment towards women. Many females are solely used for sexual pleasure, talked down too, abused, misused and blamed for their emotional issues. All of which express a mindset that hinders us from showing them the Love that their Heavenly Father wants them to receive from us.

So, if we are to truly express God's love for our women, there will be times we will need the strength of His Grace to be different on purpose from the other selfish males around us. There will come a time where you will have the opportunity to express love and kindness while other guys are being selfish and lustful. If you are to express the light of His love during these times, you will need

His Grace to be different on purpose and He will provide it to you if you really want it.

Grace To Restore

Based on the negative statistics on how many women are mistreated and experience some form of abuse from a male, you will undoubtedly come in contact with a female, either young or old, that has been mistreated or abused, that you know nothing about.

It's during this time, that you can receive God's Grace to help restore some areas of hurt that she may have experienced or that she may currently be experiencing. This doesn't mean that you will say or do something that immediately brings a form of healing to her. It may be a simple kind word, or your loving nature, that helps to heal her in an area of pain that she may have experienced.

You may not be used to bring complete healing in an instant. But you can allow God's Grace to flow through you in such a way that it can help begin the process of restoration and healing that neither you or her realize is taking place, simply because the love of God on your life, is impacting her life by Grace. You never know what a kind word or smile will do for someone else in need.

Grace To Replace

Along those same lines as Grace to Restore, let's discuss Grace to Replace what was done by the enemy, with the help of God's love and power. John 10:10 NIV says, **_"The thief comes only to steal, and kill and destroy; I have come that they may have life and have it to the full."_**

If you truly let God's Grace to love others flow through your life, He will allow your path to cross with people that the enemy has or is trying to destroy so that they can experience His love through you. He will use you to replace the evil that the enemy has done to them, or is planning for them, with His love that you've connected to by His Grace.

Grace To Impact

When we think about Jesus and His Disciples, a few men, with God's Power and Grace, changed the known world. The Son of God, walked on Earth for 33 years and changed the entire course of society and creation. Even people that don't accept or believe that Jesus Christ is the Son of God, live by a calendar that is counting down from his birth and death.

Even the terms "A.D." and "B.C." have their roots in the life of Jesus Christ. The term "A.D." stands for "**anno domini**" (Latin for "in the year of the lord"), and it refers specifically to the birth of Jesus Christ. While the term "B.C." stands for "**before Christ**.", or the time on Earth before the birth of Jesus. [7] So Jesus Christ walked in so much Grace that His impact changed the entire world.

As a son of God that walks in His Love, you can walk in the Grace of God that Impacts the world around you. This Grace should have a positive impact on your woman, your wife, your family and others. Just make a conscious effort to express God's Love to everyone you come in contact with, and His Grace to impact the world around you will flow through your life.

Grace To Love

And finally, on the topic of Grace, let's discuss the Grace to Love. 1 Corinthians 13:13 NIV says, "**_And now these three remain: faith, hope and love. But the greatest of these is love._**" From this verse, we summarize that love is one of the most important aspects of the Christian lifestyle. I believe that love is so important because it opens the door and gives access to all the other gifts and abilities that we will need to express God's love and Kingdom here on Earth.

Romans 5:6 NLT says, "_**When we were utterly helpless, Christ came at just the right time and died for us sinners.**_" So, God's Grace is available and working for us whether we are using and responding to it or not. God's love is flowing to us all the time whether we recognize or receive it. It's also flowing to those that may not even want it.

Matthew 5:45 NIV says, "_**...He causes his sun to rise on the evil and the good, and sends rain on the righteous and the unrighteous.**_" God's Love isn't limited solely to those who accept Jesus Christ or even believe in Him as God. His love is currently flowing to all mankind. But that may not always be the case.

Sir Isaac Newton's Third Law of Motion: Action & Reaction states, "**Whenever one object exerts a force on a second object, the second object exerts an equal and opposite force on the first. Or that, for every action (force) in nature there is an equal and opposite reaction.**" [8] So in essence, what is done in one direction is matched in the opposite direction.

However, when it comes to God's love, He gives without needing to receive. His love flows from Him towards those who may never return His love to Him and never acknowledge that it's even there. Despite that, His love still flows towards us without losing strength or passion.

However, for us to truly love with His kind of Love we must have His Grace to do so. If we try and love with our own strength or ability, we will get tired and drained if the love we give away isn't returned back to us. But if we love with God's love, we will never run out, never get exhausted and never stop because His love never ends. And if we truly love with His Love it'll never run out because it's not our love in the first place.

If we use God's Grace to Love our wives, our children and others, even when the situations or circumstances change, our love will remain consistent and pure. We won't be able to do that without the Grace of God to Love flowing through our lives.

Question for You

In what areas do you need more Grace from God to be a man of love? Have you asked for it yet?

A GIFT TO MEN

Then the LORD God said, "It is not good for the man to be alone. I will make a helper who is just right for him." ~Genesis 2:18 NLT

If God is Good, and what He does is Good, and what He gives is Good, then God giving a woman to a man is Good. It's not about whether or not we understand it at face value. If you understand the essence of the giver, which is God, then you understand the essence of the gift, which is Good.

Now, with that said, let's discuss why a Woman is a Gift from a Loving Father.

His Garden

When it comes to men understanding and loving women, it would probably be wise to listen to a man that has had a lot of experience in that area, like King Solomon. King Solomon is the one person that every guy needs to personally find in Heaven to ask him one simple and important question, "What were you thinking?!"

1 Kings 11 verses 2, 3 from the NIV say, "*...You must not intermarry with them, because they will surely turn your hearts after their gods.*"

Nevertheless, Solomon held fast to them in love. He had seven hundred wives of royal birth and three hundred concubines, and his wives led him astray." Solomon's love for, and attraction to women led him away from following the commands of God.

What is it about women that drew the wisest and wealthiest man alive, away from the commands of the God that gave him the wisdom, and wealth, in the first place? To further address this question lets quickly lists 3 of the most sensual verses I've found in the Bible.

Isaiah 66:11 says, "That you may nurse and be satisfied with her comforting breasts, that you may suck and be delighted with her bountiful bosom."

Song of Solomon 4:5 says, "Your two breasts are like two fawns, twins of a gazelle which feed among the lilies"

Song of Solomon 7:8 says, "I said, 'I will climb the palm tree, I will take hold of its fruit stalks. Oh, may your breasts be like clusters of the vine, and the fragrance of your breath like apples"

At the end of the day, Solomon was smitten by the essence of what a woman is. And since he had so, so many of them, I don't think it was just one woman in particular that drew him. It was the essence of what God has given men in the many different shapes, sizes, races, personalities, etc. of what women have been created to be. All of these exciting and attractive women are what drew him from the commandments of God.

And if we're honest, God knew that what He made in women was good, attractive and alluring, which is why He gave the commandment in the first place to "NOT" be drawn away by them because they will draw you to their foreign gods, their foreign beliefs and their foreign practices.

In essence, what I'm saying is that a woman has been designed by God to receive from a man and return to him what he gives her. We as men are drawn to the fruit of a woman, because that's how good God created them. It's the devil's job to make us hurl, abuse and disrespect their garden so that we don't receive the good harvest from them that God wants us to receive. The enemy wants guys to receive back evil from the garden of our women instead of good because of the evil that guys plant into their ground.

<u>His Return</u>

Luke 6:38 (NIV) says, ***"Give, and it will be given to you. A good measure, pressed down, shaken together and running over, will be poured into your lap. For with the measure you use, it will be measured to you."***

Now if you are with me in understanding that your woman is your garden, let me ask you three simple but important questions:

- #1: If you understand that she's your garden, what type of seeds are you sowing into her?
- #2: What do you want her to return to you? Good or Bad?
- #3: Do you actually have good seeds in your own heart and mind to sow into her?

One day, a guy I know was complaining about his wife. He said to me, "She keeps asking me where I'm going? Who will I be with? When will I be back? It's getting on my nerves!" Being the great friend I am, I let him talk until he was done. Now a little back story, he had already cheated on her, more than once and she was still with him, which was a miracle from Heaven in my humble opinion.

After he had let it all out, I reminded him that he had cheated, betrayed confidence, acted selfishly, broken his covenant with God and that he didn't seem to know in what woman's vagina his penis belonged in. A little harsh I know, but he was getting on my nerves at this point. So, it was time for some For Real, in YO Face, Brotherly Love!

I then told him, "Only a child gets caught doing wrong and then complains about the punishment they get,". She is wondering what you are doing now because of what you did then! So, whose fault is that? Hers or yours? He didn't really like that because I smacked him in the mouth with the truth, but he had to stop complaining about what she was doing without taking responsibility for what he had done.

So, to every man, God has given us the ability to determine our return based on the seeds we sow into the women we say we love.

His Legacy

Psalm 128:3 (NIV) says, *"__Your wife will be like a fruitful vine within your house; your children will be like olive shoots around your table.__"*

We talked earlier about the islands and the one with the man and woman being filled with kids if left uninterrupted for years. One of the gifts I believe God has given men is the ability to create a lasting and fruitful legacy by partnering with women that they love and having children with them that allowed their essence to last far beyond their initial years on earth.

God told Abraham in Genesis 22:17 (NIV), *"__I will surely bless you and make your descendants as numerous as the stars in the sky and as the sand on the seashore. Your descendants will take possession of the cities of their enemies,__"* God promised Abraham a legacy that would far extend him. But this legacy was not going to happen without Abraham's wife. Every man/husband has the ability to join with a woman/wife and create a lasting legacy that far outlives him on the Earth.

Unfortunately, some guys destroy that legacy by abusing their wives, hurting their children, being too stubborn to change or never admitting and apologizing for their faults. So even though they have children, their children want nothing to do with them.

To further express this point, I would like to share a post from "Ministry127.com" which stated: *"Executives of a greeting-card company decided to do something special for Mother's Day. They set up a table in a federal prison, inviting inmates to send a free card to their Mom. The lines were so long they had to get more cards. Due to the success of that event, they decided to do the same thing on Father's Day, but this time, not one prisoner felt the need to send a card to his Dad. In fact, when asked about it, many had no idea who their fathers were. [9]*

I share this simple example to express how many guys are losing contact with their wives, children and legacy. This is NOT God's will and can be repaired if we as men learn to love our women and children God's way.

Question

Do you see women as Gifts from God? If you do, in what ways do you express that in how you love and treat them?

FYI...please keep in mind that if you don't see them as Gifts, the "Gift Giver" will respond on their behalf. You've been warned.

Love is not enough.
It must be the foundation,
the cornerstone - but not the
complete structure. It is
much too pliable, too
yielding.

~ Bette Davis

PART 3:
UNDERSTANDING

Wisdom is the principle thing; therefore, get wisdom and in all thy getting, get understanding ~ Proverbs 4:7

A doctor is not a doctor because he wants to be. A licensed, registered and professional doctor is so because he or she has taken the time to study, train and be trained and apply the principles and knowledge of human anatomy, the latest medical breakthroughs, medicine, circulatory systems and may other things that I'm not knowledgeable enough about to list here.

In the same way, a man does not know how to automatically love, honor and respect a woman on his own. As boys we are selfish, childish and often very lustful; none of which will create a lasting relationship with a woman.

If we want to truly love and honor women, we must understand how.

UNFRUITFUL WORKS

"Take no part in the unfruitful works of darkness, but instead expose them." ~Ephesians 5:11 ESV

Something to always keep in mind is that every action you take will either enhance or harm your life in some way. So, if everything you do in life has an effect, some actions will be fruitful and improve your life while others will be unfruitful and worsen it.

So, let's discuss of few of the unfruitful acts that we as men take when it comes to our women and why they are unfruitful in our lives.

Empty Pursuits

empty [emp-tee] noun - containing nothing; having none of the usual or appropriate contents: having no occupant or occupants; vacant; unoccupied:

How many times have you chased after something that provided a temporary pleasure, but no long-lasting benefit? The problem with empty pursuits is that most of the time, we aren't able to recognize them until we have matured enough to evaluate them or someone else points them out for us.

So, with that said, for a Christ-centered guy, an "Empty Pursuit" is: *"Any thought, word or activity that when compared to the Kingdom of God and the finished works of Jesus, will amount to nothing and cause us to lose a Heavenly Reward."* For a Christ centered guy, and Empty Pursuit is anything that doesn't express to the World that he is a member of the Kingdom of God and that he's walking in the finished works of Jesus Christ.

1 Corinthians 3:10-15 NIV says, *"By the grace God has given me, I laid a foundation as a wise builder, and someone else is building on it. But each one should build with care. For no one can lay any foundation other than the one already laid, which is Jesus Christ. If anyone builds on this foundation using gold, silver, costly stones, wood, hay or straw, their work will be shown for what it is, because the Day will bring it to light. It will be revealed with fire, and the fire will test the quality of each person's work. If what has been built survives, the builder will receive a reward. If it is burned up, the builder will suffer loss but yet will be saved—even though only as one escaping through the flames."*

This verse that Paul shared expresses that his life and works are laying a foundation for something.

And this foundation he is laying will either last or be burned up. If every Christian is called to live a life that expresses The Kingdom of God, then every Christian is building on the foundation that was laid by Jesus Christ in some way. So, if what we build on His foundation is not based in the Love of God, it will probably be burned up, even if we make it into Heaven.

If a person builds on the foundation that Jesus left for us and what they add to that foundation is burned up, how will that effect their reward? If they are forgiven for all their sins by Grace, but there's no record of what they've done, because their life on Earth was filled with empty pursuits, how will that effect their life in Heaven?

Ok, the rabbit hole is getting deeper and deeper, so I'll stop. The point is, I think every Christian guy should strive to avoid "Empty Pursuits" that have no Heavenly benefit in their lives, either now on earth, or in the future in Heaven. So, here's a quick list of what I think Empty pursuits are. Each one would probably extend this book another 25 pages each so I will just list them here and probably make YouTube videos about them in the future.

So, here's my quick list of a few Empty Pursuits:
- Sex without Commitment
- Taking without Giving
- Disrespectful Words and Acts
- Abuse of Any Kind
- Words Meant to Hurt
- Acts of Anger
- Blame and Accusations
- Negative Talk
- Doubt and Fear

Most of us will probably have experienced one and performed at least one or more of these Empty Pursuits, I know I have. But the goal is not to make any of them a lifestyle. As Christ-centered men, we need to learn, repent and grow, so that the life we live builds a foundation that will last.

Excuses, Excuses, Excuses

excuse [ik-skyoos] noun - an explanation offered to be omitted from or to avoid the consequences of a thing or situation; a reason to release from an obligation or duty.

I don't know about you, but one of the most sorry things I've ever seen a man do is not except responsibility for his own actions. A guy that always makes excuses for why he did what he did, why he should be allowed to do what he did and why it's someone else's fault is a sad state of affairs in my opinion. If all you do is make excuses for what you have or don't have, you'll never come up with the solution and plan necessary to get you the things you want, the things you need or the things you deserve.

When it comes to loving a woman, making excuses for why you are not honoring her, for why you disrespect her or for why it's not your fault is pathetic in my opinion for any man of quality. Excuses are for weak little boys that don't want to do better or be better for the women and the children that need them.

So don't make excuses. Except responsibility and make the necessary adjustments to be the quality man you need to be for the woman and children you say you love.

Social Norms

norm [nawrm] noun - a standard, model, or pattern - a behavior pattern or trait considered typical of a particular social group:

Social norms are those things that we've become accustomed to seeing or doing in our society. But just because it's normal or expected, doesn't make it right, especially when it comes to the Kingdom of God. Social norms are those things that the un-renewed mind, or an un-renewed society accepts as right. Just because the people around you or the society around you accepts an activity, mindset, belief, or lifestyle as normal doesn't make it right and shouldn't make it normal in a Christians life.

Hebrews 13:8-9 NIV says, ***"Jesus Christ is the same yesterday and today and forever. Do not be carried away by all kinds of strange teachings..."*** God, His Son Jesus Christ and Holy Spirit have not changed, and neither has the essence of what makes a successful human being.

What has changed is our viewpoints, technology and our understanding of the world around us. But the love, kindness, affection, safety and protection that our women need to feel happy from the men in their lives is still the same.

If you really want to love and honor your woman, don't allow the social norms that make it easy for a man to use, abuse and mistreat a woman become acceptable behavior in your life just because it's what other selfish and immature guys do. Don't allow the negative and childish social norms of our society lead you to destroy the connection you have with your woman and family just because you don't know how to stand out and be different.

The Guy Game

game [geym] noun - an amusement or pastime - something done as a chance for stakes; to gamble.

As young boys, most guys learn to be competitive by playing what I label, "The Guy Game". This is the game that guys play against each other that make us compete on the playground, compete on sports teams and compete for women. In the Guy Game, it's the guy with the most women that stands bigger and above the other guys.

The problem with "The Guy Game" is that it diminishes the importance of our women and makes them more like items to possess and flaunt, instead of equals that we love and protect. Guys that live by "The Guy Game" are constantly talking about how many women they have been with, what they did with them last night and who's the next one on their list. The Guy Game makes women a conquest that gets replaced every time the conquest is complete.

If you have ever operated in the Guy Game, I strongly suggest you do as I did and change your mind about how you love and honor women. Women are not just items to be used for sex and pleasure. They are meant to be loved and honored. If you are operating in the Guy Game now, or have operated in it at some time in the past, please repent and withdraw from the game.

The word "repent" is not only defined as *"to feel sorrow or regret"*, but also as, *"to change your mind and your direction"*. So, if you truly want to be a man of honor that pleases God in the way you treat His daughters and the women you come in contact with. Don't let the selfishness of The Guy Game keep you from walking in the true power and blessing that God has for you.

Unforgiven Ex's

forgive [fer-giv] verb - to grant pardon for or remission of (an offense, debt, etc.); absolve - to cease to feel resentment against:

One of the most important mindsets for every Christian to operate in is forgiveness. Matthew 6:14-15 (KJV) says, ***"For if ye forgive men their trespasses, your heavenly Father will also forgive you: But if ye forgive not men their trespasses, neither will your Father forgive your trespasses."*** So, I don't know about you guys, but there have been some women I have loved and really cared for, that cheated on me, that didn't honor me, that didn't know how to talk to me and in general didn't treat me with the kindness I treated them with.

So, in these cases, I've had to forgive these ex's to make sure that I didn't carry the hurt they caused me in my heart, so that I didn't give hurt to another woman that she didn't deserve. When it comes to us as guys, we must learn to forgive the past mistakes women have made, no matter how wrong or destructive their actions were. It's a waste of time to hold on to them and self destructive in the long term.

Don't spend your time talking about how crazy or selfish women were in your past. Instead, spend your time focusing on the woman you have now, or will have in the future, and how you can love her the way God wants you too today. If you do, He'll reward you for how you treat His daughter. I'm certain of it!

Destructive Identities

identity [ahy-den-ti-tee] noun - condition or character as to who a person or what a thing is; the qualities, beliefs, etc., that distinguish or identify a person or thing - A sense or understanding that someone adopts as their own

There're several messages being presented to guys on how we should treat our women and children. These messages embody several different types of identities that a guy can take. Don't believe me? Just pay attention to the types of identities that are shown in movies, music, social media and TV shows. How often have you seen messages of abuse, racism, murder, greed, pride, selfishness.

In every message there's a choice to become what you see or to reject it. Now of course, most of these movies have a hero that wins out in the end, but seeing the hero win in the end, doesn't replace the negative messages and identities that were shown. Some of these identities may be considered good and positive, while others may be destructive and hurtful.

For example, during a holiday, my family and I went to see a comedy movie where the main character took up boxing to help the kids at his school. We took a few of my mother's foster children with us, and as soon as we got to the car and I pulled off, I turned back to see my little foster brother punching the back seat just like the character from the movie. He immediately took on the identity of a boxer and hopefully a hero.

To consider the effects of what we watch from the other side, the website "**fightthenewdrug.org**" shared a post that stated, *"In one study of fraternity men, those who consumed mainstream pornography expressed a greater intent to commit rape if they knew they would not be caught than those who did not consume pornography."* [10]

In the same post they also shared, *"Additionally, those who consumed sadomasochistic pornography expressed significantly less willingness to intervene in situations of sexual violence, greater belief in rape myths, and greater intent to commit rape, and among those who consumed rape-themed pornography, the researchers described "serious effects" including less bystander willingness to intervene and greater intent to commit rape."* [11] My personal story, along with the commentary from this article, hopefully shares a perspective on how what we watch impacts our identity.

So, if you want to truly love and honor your woman, it's vital that you don't accept into your heart, or mind, any identity that will cause hurt to her or to your relationship with her. Proverbs 23:7 says, **_"For as he thinketh in his heart, so is he:"_** So, always recognize the messages around you and what identity they're trying to get you to accept as your own. Every destructive identity that will lead to dishonor, disrespect or destruction should be avoided at all costs!

Repeated Disrespect

disrespect [dis-ri-spekt] verb to regard or treat without respect; regard or treat with contempt or rudeness. - lack of respect; discourtesy; rudeness.

Continuing along the lines of destructive identities, it's important to understand that a destructive identity will lead you towards actions of disrespect. These can be things that you do either in her presence, or behind her back. Destructive identities care very little for others or their feelings and inevitably damage, and in many cases destroy the relationship you have with your woman and others.

Continued disrespect is a surefire way to push the woman away from you that you say you love and create a wedge between you two. Also, if you justify the disrespect, you show her it expresses your own personal immaturity and maybe quite frankly your inability to know how to cherish and to care for the woman that God has allowed to be in your presence.

For example, are you one of those guys that always blame the woman for the issues in your relationship? Is it always her fault, is she always too emotional? Does she never understand you and your perspective? If that's the case, then quite frankly I have a question for you and that's why are you in a relationship in the first place? And who actually taught you how to be a man that deserves to be in relationship with the woman that you say you love?

If you find yourself repeatedly disrespecting your woman by the words you speak, by the actions you take, by the way you treat her, either in or out of her presence, you will inevitably end up alone because of you're repeated disrespect. So, if being alone is what you want, being alone is what you will get, and being alone is what you deserve if disrespect is a part of your life.

<u>No Accountability</u>

accountability [uh-koun-tuh-bil-i-tee] noun - the state of being accountable, liable, or answerable:

Every person that wants to live in integrity and success needs someone or something that they submit to and is accountable to. A person that's not accountable to any person, any standards or any principles, is liable to do anything. A person that is accountable knows that there is someone or something to help them keep their life, their decisions, and their standards in order.

Consider this, what if the typical individual didn't have a boss at work or any rules to follow? They had complete freedom regarding when and how they came to work, left, and took breaks, and they continued to get paid. But if this was the case, how much work would really be done? This is why organizations have a structure in place to make sure that everyone is effective in their particular job so that the overall goal of the organization is carried out.

So, when it comes to your life and how you treat your woman, who are you accountable to? There's an old saying that says, "What happens in this house, stays in this house." I actually don't like that saying because what if abuse is happening in that house, what if children are being molested or abused? What if the devil is literally having a field day in that house? Should that not be shared? How will the wife or children get help?

If you're a Christ follower, you are accountable to treating the woman and children in your life with love and honor. You are accountable and required by their Heavenly Father to protect them from evil from within you and from outside the home. Having no one and nothing that holds you accountable to love and honor leaves you open to allowing negative thoughts to become destructive actions because there's no one to help judge them.

Find someone to help you be accountable to being a quality man of character and love!

Denying The Power

deny [dih-nahy] verb - to refuse to agree or accede to - to refuse to recognize or acknowledge; disown; disavow; repudiate:

For guys who have received Jesus Christ as Lord and Savior, His Grace is available to help us love and honor His Daughters and our women as He would. If a Christian guy doesn't show women and children love and honor, he's rejecting the grace and power that Jesus Christ paid for him to have with His shed blood.

2 Timothy 3:2-7 talks about the types of people that reject what Jesus has done for them: ***"For men shall be lovers of their own selves, covetous, boasters, proud, blasphemers, disobedient to parents, unthankful, unholy.***

Without natural affection, trucebreakers, false accusers, incontinent, fierce, despisers of those that are good, Traitors, heady, highminded, lovers of pleasures more than lovers of God; Having a form of godliness, but denying the power thereof: from such turn away. For of this sort are they which creep into houses, and lead captive silly women laden with sins, led away with divers lusts, Ever learning, and never able to come to the knowledge of the truth."

If you claim to be a Son of God, through the Shed Blood of Jesus, you have been given the opportunity to connect to the Power of God that's available to help you, love instead of hate, to lift instead of destroy and help instead of hurt. And if you don't know how to do that, it's done by faith. Just ask God to help you and He will. You'll be surprised how much He will come to help you show His Love to the woman in your life.

Why? Well, because He loves her much more than you ever could, so let Him show you His power that's available for you. I know it sounds easy, that's because it is.

<u>Not Expressing Him</u>

express [ik-spres] verb - to show, manifest, or reveal - to clearly indicate or distinctly state

Let's be honest. People can get on your nerves. People can be rude, arrogant, mean, selfish, hateful and all around unpleasant. And if we're even more honest, we have all had times when we are just as rude, selfish, arrogant, mean, etc as the next person.

As Christ followers, our lives shouldn't be solely focused on us. Our lives should express the fact that we were bought with the Shed Blood of Jesus. Because of that, we are no longer living for ourselves only, but we live as expressions of what He has done for us. Our actions and our lives should show the world that we are different from the regular un-renewed person living for themselves and pursuing their own selfish goals.

If you are not showing love to the woman and gift in your life, you're NOT expressing God. 1 John 4:7-8 (KJV) says, "***Beloved, let us love one another, for love is from God, has been born of God and knows God. Anyone who does not love does not know God, because God is love.***

If you desire to be a Son of God, you want people around you to truly experience God by the way you treat them. You may be the only Light that some people will ever come in contact with. When it comes to your wife, I again want to stress how much of a privilege every man has to purposely love her with God's love and receive a reward from God for doing so.

It's the devil's plan to have every guy turn against his woman and family and not love them, to abuse them, to disrespect them, to hurt them and to eventually loose them. Just like John 10:10 (NIV) says, *"__The thief comes only to steal and kill and destroy; I have come that they may have life, and have it to the full.__"*

Don't let the thief, the enemy, the devil *"__steal__"* the atmosphere of love you can create with your woman. Then don't let him *"__kill__"* the potential for life that you have with her. And finally, don't let him *"__destroy__"* the future and destiny that you can create with her and her only.

What's one of the best ways to make sure this does not happen? Make a decision to purposely express God's love to her and to everyone you come in contact with. If you really want to show the love of God to others, when you do mess up or step outside of your love circle, Holy Spirit will be there to help you to repent, make adjustments and get back on track towards the purpose and plan of God in your life.

Question

Have you performed any of these unfruitful acts with a woman that you "say" you loved? If so, how did that work out for you?

THE 3 A'S OF ALONE

"It is better to dwell in a corner of the housetop, than with a brawling woman [or brawling man] in a wide house." ~Proverbs 21:9 KJV

A friend of mine said something one day that I thought was awesome. I'm not sure if he made it up, or if he got it from somebody else, but I would like to share it here.

He said, "There's 3 things a woman should never put up with: Abuse, Adultery and Addiction." I've adjusted that quote into a group I've titled, "**The 3 A's of Alone**" because if you do these to your woman, you'll end up alone, eventually! Even if she's sitting next to you on the couch, she may not actually be with you. You may be in her presence, but still alone. You just may be too blind to notice.

So, let's discuss each one quickly:

#1: Abuse

abuse [uh-byooz] - verb
to use wrongly or improperly; to treat in a harmful, injurious, or offensive way; to speak insultingly, harshly, and unjustly to or about.

When a man abuses a woman, either mentally, sexually and/or physically, he damages not just her, but the way he relates to her and the way she relates to him. He purposely, and by his own actions, destroys the connection and the trust between them.

Think about this: *"What would happen if you purposely, walked up to the most important apple tree in your garden and kicked it, chopped at it, smacked it, burned it and abused it?"* Eventually, your once lovely apple tree would no longer be able to provide you with its life-giving fruit because of the mistreatment and abuse it received from your own hands.

Any man that abuses a woman, destroys his ability to receive life-giving fruit from her in the form of her wisdom, her support, her kindness, her love, her understanding and her affection.

#2: Adultery

adultery [uh-duhl-tuh-ree] - noun
voluntary sexual intercourse between a married person and someone other than their lawful spouse.

Mark 10:8-9 NKJV says, "***...and the two shall become one flesh'; so then they are no longer two,*** *but one flesh. Therefore what God has joined together, let not man separate."*

Sexual intercourse is much more than a one-time quick and pleasing experience. When a man and a woman join together, two separate physical and sexual areas fit together to become one. When "**His Giving Member**" joins with "**Her Receiving Area**", a oneness and connection is created that's both physical and spiritual.

So, when a husband joins himself with another person other than his wife, he breaks the oneness he had with her and creates a new oneness with another woman. This is why a woman/man has a right to leave his/her spouse in the case of adultery. By joining with another person sexually, they've replaced the physical connection they had with their spouse and created a new one with someone else.

In doing so, they have decided to separate from their spouse and have created a new connection with someone else that may only be temporary and may eventually cause them to end up alone.

#3: Addiction

addiction [uh-dik-shuhn] - noun

the state of being compulsively committed to a habit, practice, substance or something that is habit-forming either psychologically or physically;

When a guy is addicted to something, that impulsive desire has the ability to override other areas and relationships in his life. Addictions are personal and can easily become the focus of someone's life. So, when a guy has an addiction to anything instead of his wife and family, that addiction will most likely lead him to do things that will destroy not just his relationships but possibly the lives of those around him.

This is why addictions are so destructive to relationships. When someone is addicted to something it can become their god and replace all other quality relationships in their life.

Question

Have you ever had a challenge, or struggled with, any of the 3 A's of Alone?

If so, what are you doing to make sure that none of the 3 A's of Alone will damage any of your current relationships?

THE EFFECTS OF DISHONOR

"Love is an irresistible desire to be irresistibly desired."
~ Robert Frost

When males don't have the proper respect and honor for women, the damage they cause extends far beyond one act of dishonor. It can span generations. A guy who grows up thinking less of women and treats them with disrespect will pass his negative thought process down to his children and any guys that watch or follow him. While on the other side, a woman who's mistreated by men will most likely experience great emotional pain and share that pain and disappointment with other women, younger girls and her own daughter. She is also much more likely to develop negative opinions and beliefs about males, based on her experiences. So, let's talk about the different types of effects that are created when males don't honor women.

On Your Relationships

In the beginning of a relationship between a man and a woman, the immediate effect of dishonor happens to her heart. The saying is true that what you give, you shall receive. As the head of a relationship, when a man gives honor and love into his wife's life, he receives willing love, honor and respect in return from her. A woman that's dishonored will not feel secure in who she is to him and in the relationship, she has with him.

On Your Thinking

The effects on a woman's immediate thinking, when she doesn't receive honor and love in her relationships, will affect how she thinks about herself. A woman who truly loves her man or husband wants to please him, and when she is not treated well, she may think of herself as a failure which may cause other issues like sadness or depression.

On the other side, a man who doesn't see the importance of honor for women may experience failed relationship after failed relationship without ever seeing himself as the primary cause because he never understood the importance of the honor he failed to give the women in his life.

On Your Emotions

The effect of dishonor on a woman's immediate emotions will vary. A strong woman will know she doesn't deserve the dishonor she receives, and it will anger her. From those emotions she may argue, break things, cheat on him and eventually leave him.

Sometimes a man cheats because he's insecure and doesn't appreciate what he has at home and he's too immature to understand the importance of faithfulness. While a woman may cheat based on what she used to get from the relationship but isn't getting any longer or maybe what she never really had. But cheating under any circumstance is still wrong, but there's always a reason.

Once a woman becomes empty emotionally, she will begin to long for what she is missing. This is most likely a loss of attention and affection. For either the male or female to dishonor their relationship is wrong. However, males and females, often have completely different emotional points of origin and reasons for when they are unfaithful or dishonorable.

On Your Conversations

When people experience hurt and dishonor, it affects their conversations and perspective. For example, when a person's feelings are hurt, they'll normally speak from the perspective of their hurt feelings. Most people speak from their experiences first.

It takes a very mature person to be able to see both sides of an issue while experiencing hurt. So, most subsequent conversations a woman has will be a result of how she's treated.

While if the man doesn't take responsibility enough to honor her, he will do all he can to take the focus off him and put it on her. He may blame her for being too sensitive, or for imagining things just to get the focus off him and back on her. These types of back-and-forth conversations can be avoided when honor is given in the relationship and to the feelings that both the male and female are experiencing.

<u>On New Relationships</u>

Both males and females should always take the time to heal after ending a painful relationship, before starting a new one. When people jump from one painful relationship to another, they will most likely take the hurt from the past relationship into the new one.

When we take old hurts and feelings into new relationships, we can easily cause the new relationship to suffer based on the effects of an old one. When women aren't honored in one relationship, they'll most likely take those feelings and experiences into their new relationship, especially if she hasn't taken the time to heal.

On Your Future Conflicts

Some conflicts happen in a new relationship because of how a person was treated in the old one. If a woman hasn't taken the time to heal from the previous relationship, she may bring in a degree of fear and accusation into the new relationship based on past mistreatment.

Sometimes a man who is right in his intentions toward a woman, may not be able to maintain a new relationship with her because of how she was treated in a past relationship. Every man that dishonors a woman creates possible obstacles and conflicts for the next man that encounters her.

So, it's important that every quality man make the most of every opportunity he has to have a positive impact on a woman.

<u>On Your Thoughts & Ideas</u>

Another reason a man should honor a woman is if she is mistreated enough it may begin to affect the way she thinks about herself and about males in general. If a woman continues to receive dishonor and mistreatment, she may begin to think, "All men are dogs," "There are no good men out there," or even worse she may begin to think, "I must deserve this somehow." None of these are true; however, if she's mistreated enough, her thoughts and ideas may begin to try and justify the dishonor she continues to receive.

She may also begin to share her ideas about why she was treated with dishonor, whether they are true or not. This is another reason why males must learn to be mindful of how we treat the women we are honored to have in our lives because we never know what impact our dishonor will have on them or others.

Question

Have you ever labeled a woman a "b@*tch"? Would you want that label used to describe your mother, sister or daughter? If your answer is no, should you ever use that word yourself?

MISCONCEPTIONS

"To love deeply in one direction makes us more loving in all others." ~Anne-Sophie Swetchine

Here are a few misconceptions that get in the way when it comes to the ways males relate to females. They are just that, misconceptions. Let's discuss just a few of them.

The Weakness Of Women

Women may be weaker, in many cases, in physical strength than men; however, they are not weak in any way. She may not be able to bench-press 240lbs, however, she can adjust her body to allow another human being to form in her womb and push that new human life out of her body after nine months. That's what you call true strength!

Males need to understand that women weren't made weaker or lesser in importance or real strength, they have different strengths and abilities so that males and females can share the load towards the common goals of family, marriage and the advancement of the human race.

I actually believe that the reason God made women physically weaker in strength is for the benefit of men. Why you ask? Well, think about this: How powerful is it for a man to use his strength to care for his woman? If she was as strong as him, she wouldn't need his care.

This is why a true man never abuses a woman. It's because he understands that his strength is to benefit her not to hurt, harm or take advantage of her but to be a blessing to her if she allows him.

A Man Leads From The Front

One thing that males seem to get mixed up a lot is what it means to really love and lead a woman. Ephesians 5:25 - 28 in the Message Translation of the Bible says, "**_Husbands, go all out in your love for your wives, exactly as Christ did for the church—a love marked by giving, not getting._**" Men often think that as the head, he makes the rules and orders the house around.

However, in God's eyes, the job of the head is to set the tone of the house as the leader that shows everyone else what it means to live and operate by God's principles and standards. When a man loves as the Bible instructs, his love is designed to protect first and receive last.

To lead a woman in honor is to make decisions that are designed to help her, designed to love her and designed to protect her. I didn't say that every decision was right or even effective, but if they are made from a sincere hearts desire to show love, a woman would have an easier time submitting to them because she knows her man loves her and wants the best for her and their relationship.

As the leader, a man should lead in love and honor. If the head is not showing love and honor in the house, how can the other members who are supposed to be under him show love? The man should set the standard for the whole and will be held accountable for its success and its failure.

There's Something Wrong With Women

I think it would be safe to say that either you've said, thought or heard another guy complain about a woman in some way. There's a mentality that I think many guys have that says, "Women are weird; They are too emotional; They always blame the man; etc." I personally disagree with these viewpoints that place blame on women for one simple reason. That reason is, "God made women to be loved, honored, respected and our partners and He doesn't make mistakes."

The point is not that there's something "wrong" with women. The point is we need to understand how God made them and love them the way He designed them to be loved. Guys need to stop blaming women for our lack of understanding and take the time to ask the Creator for help on how to love and honor His Creation the way He wants them loved and honored.

1 Peter 3:7 AMP says, ***"In the same way, you husbands, live with your wives in an understanding way [with great gentleness and tact, and with an intelligent regard for the marriage relationship], as with someone physically weaker, since she is a woman. Show her honor and respect as a fellow heir of the grace of life, so that your prayers will not be hindered or ineffective."***

I like this particular translation because it stresses something that I think a lot of guys choose to ignore, "understanding". Many guys are quick to assume they know what their women needs and that what she says isn't really what she needs. Instead of seeking to understand his woman, he applies his selfish and incomplete perspectives on how he should treat her and then wonders why she's empty and upset.

There's absolutely nothing wrong with how God made women. It's our job as Sons of God to seek His wisdom on how to love our individual wives so that they feel loved and valued.

This is something we can't do without help and understanding from her Heavenly Father.

Question

Where did you learn how to treat a woman?

Was it from a "Quality Man" or source that had good relationships with women or just some dude running his mouth?

He who is in love is wise and is becoming wiser, sees newly every time he looks at the object beloved, drawing from it with his eyes and his mind those virtues which it possesses.

~ Ralph Waldo Emerson

PART 4:
APPLICATION

But don't just listen to God's word. You must do what it says. Otherwise, you are only fooling yourselves. ~James 1:22 NLV

Ok, so up to this point we've talked about a lot of different concepts and topics with the overall goal of being better "Christ-Centered" men that love and honor our women and our children. Now let's talk about how to actually apply these concepts to how we treat them in our everyday lives.

With that's said, I'd like to share a revelation I had. One day I was explaining to someone what the CENTRY brand is meant to be. I shared with them that it's a Christian Brand that wants to create images and concepts to help guys "Serve, Honor & Protect". They then proceeded to say, "*Are you sure you wanna tell people you're a Christian? Christians have been getting a bad rep recently. I'm just saying.*"

Now of course, that was her opinion, and it doesn't apply to every Christian on the planet, but it did make me think. One of my favorite Christian

111

rappers named "Andy Mineo" has a lyric in one of his songs that says, *"I might just tro a Buddha round my necklace....Dat Boy Reckless! Everybody rocking Jesus pieces. I'm just doing, wat y'all doing, wearing stuff I don't believe in...Yup!"*

That lyric is both hilarious and deep to me. There are people, both in and out of the Body of Christ, that walk around wearing Crosses and claiming to be Christians but don't express the love of Christ to the world around them. So instead of simply labeling myself a Christian, I am a Christ follower. As a Christ follower, I make it a point to follow Christ, not the world or the thoughts of society. I follow Christ and those that are following Christ.

When it comes to being men that follow Christ, how does Christ tell us to apply love to the women and people around us?

Let's talk about it.

LADIES, WE REPENT

"When a person is uncertain in love, there is nothing easier than for him to put one and one together and to make three out of them." ~Monica Fairview

"To the mothers, we repent to you for every son that has not shown you the appreciation and gratitude you deserve as his mother.

To the sisters, we repent to you for all of the brothers that have not treated you as a special member of their family and as a gift that you are in his sister.

To the female co-workers, we repent to you for every time a male has disrespected you at work and not seen the positive impact you make upon the organization.

To the girlfriends, we repent to you for any boyfriend that has not honored you as a special gift and woman. (Word of advice... don't look for a boyfriend, wait for a husband.)

To the wives, we repent to you for all the husbands that you have made a commitment before God to love them and they have not been honorable to you or that commitment.

To all females, of all ages, all nationalities and all backgrounds, we repent to you for every act of mistreatment, dishonor, physical abuse, verbal abuse, mental abuse, sexual abuse, disrespect and dishonor that you have received from males.

You are a gift from God, worthy of honor and respect, full of compassion, talents, greatness and love that we can't do without. Never underestimate the power packed gift you are.

You are worthy of love and honor, and we pray you allow God to heal all wounds and bring you the peace and love that He has ordained for you from the beginning of time through His Son Jesus the Christ."

To Your Success...
Eric M. Watterson and
The CENTRY League, LLC

IT'S SEXUAL INTERCOURSE

For this reason, a man shall leave his father and his mother, and be joined to his wife; and they shall become one flesh. ~Genesis 2:24 NASB

We would like to take a few moments to speak about sexual intercourse. And let's be clear, we're not just talking about sex, but sexual intercourse. I think if we use the entire word, and not the shortened version, we can really place the proper impact upon the act and further clarify its place.

Our society is fascinated with quick and easy; the less work the better and instant gratification is always best. People strive for pleasure; pleasure in what they do and pleasure from what they get from others. Now, of course, pleasure in and of itself is not wrong; however, the pursuit of pleasure devoid of purpose will cause a person to end up empty inside.

Why? Pleasure by itself is temporary and lasts only for the moment, while purpose is eternal and lasts forever.

<u>**What It Is**</u>

Webster defines the word **"intercourse"** as, *"dealings or communication between individuals, groups, countries, etc. The interchange of thoughts, feelings, etc. Sexual relations or a sexual coupling; mutual dealings, and as, Connection or dealings between persons or groups".*

So, with these descriptions, it can be understood that sexual intercourse is *"the exchange between two people, not just in body but also in their hearts, in their minds and in their spirits."*

As humans, there's more to us than just our physical bodies. We're also made up of our spirits and souls which include our emotions, our beliefs and our standards. So, during sexual intercourse, the two humans or two spirit beings unite as one and exchange passions not solely through their physical bodies, but they also unite through the essence of who they are spiritually.

When a man and woman unite, they share their physical essence or bodies with each other. They also unite and share their spiritual essence, which includes their emotions, their beliefs, their strengths, their weaknesses, their perspectives and even their personal history.

Sexual intercourse gives another person access not only to your body, but access to your inner being by way of your body. So "sexual intercourse" joins you to everything another person is, what they have, how they think and what they believe, be it good or bad, right or wrong whether you want it or not. The act of joining with their body means you also join with their spirits and everything else they are.

Our society has minimized "sex" to nothing more than a physical "act" but it's much more than that!

Sexual intercourse is actually an exchange that is pleasurable for the moment but can have everlasting affects and create a lasting bond that will affect you positively or negatively depending on what type of connection was made.

What It's Not

Sexual intercourse is not meant to be the completion of a relationship, but an addition to it. It is not designed by God to fulfill a person's needs. Contrary to popular opinion, sex is not something that every person needs. Every person needs to feel intimacy, needs to feel connected and needs to feel loved.

However, we sometimes confuse our natural "need" for connection and intimacy with our "desire" for sex or sexual intercourse. Sexual intercourse without connection or intimacy is like the icing without the cake, or the gravy without the chicken. It's a great and pleasing topping, for a moment but doesn't bring total satisfaction.

This is why people who pursue sex continue to pursue it more and more because they're searching for the satisfaction and intimacy that only comes from true connection, commitment and purpose.

Where It Belongs

One reason why people spend their time pursuing sex is because they are looking for a fulfilling and meaningful relationship. For sexual intercourse to be truly fulfilling, it must be attached to a "meaningful" relationship. Without it, a person will move from sexual encounter to sexual encounter searching for a sense of true fulfillment that will only come when sexual intercourse supports a true and meaningful commitment because it's used to further create a lasting bond between a man and a woman.

Sexual intercourse does not satisfy a person's inner being but provides momentary pleasure to the physical body. The source of true happiness is internal and can't be seen by the natural eye because it's not a natural thing.

For example, the love between a mother and a child cannot be seen by the eye because it's embraced by the heart and expressed through action. With that said, sexual intercourse is meant to be an expression of the internal connection and love between a man and a woman. Without that internal connection being in place, sex may be pleasurable but never truly fulfilling.

Finally, we would like to ask that you use the words "sexual", and "intercourse" together and not use the word "sex" alone. The mere use of the word "sex" alone sounds as if it is a onetime single act with little or no lasting consequences. By using the term "sexual intercourse" we hope that it helps to magnify the importance of the act to help you to make sure that you really want to accept and connect, or intercourse, yourself with "all" that the other person has because that's exactly what will happen. Whether for the good or for the bad.

Just like you can receive a sexually transmitted disease in your body through a onetime act of sexual intercourse with the wrong person; you can also receive a disease of the mind, a disease of the heart and a disease of the spirit through sexual intercourse with the wrong person.

So please elevate your opinion and perspective about having sex. When you as a man, join your sexual member with the purposeful and God created, compatible sexual section of a woman, you both are joining everything that you both are, in mind, body and spirit into one. Sexual intercourse between a man and a woman creates something unique in the universe and should never be taken lightly.

So, make sure to only have sexual intercourse with someone that you are certain that you want to receive everything they are. Because everything they "are", is what you'll be getting!

Question

Do you think that sex is supposed to fulfill you mentally or physically?

THE MIXING OF TWO

"For this reason a man shall leave his father and his mother, and be joined to his wife; and they shall become one flesh." ~Genesis 2:24 NAS

Before we move on from the topic of Sexual Intercourse, let's spend a few moments to reinforce what happens when two separate spirits, or spiritual essences, join together. As a Christ follower, it's important that we adjust our minds and thinking to be in line with the thoughts of Christ as displayed in His word, the Holy Bible.

Ephesians 5:28 (NIV) again says, ***"In the same way, husbands ought to love their wives as they love their own bodies. For a man who loves his wife actually shows love for himself."*** So, by this scripture, we can clearly see that when a man loves his wife, the Word is saying he loves himself. So, as Men of God, it's crucial that we see as or Father sees and instead of trying to bring His Word down to our level, we need to seek the understanding to come up to His.

When a man and a woman join together in intercourse, in relationship and in marriage, they are combining not just their physical bodies but

121

their spiritual bodies. They are mixing their two unique and separate spiritual essences of man and female, to create a combined and united Spiritual Essence of both Male/Female that has never existed before and never will exist again.

At the time of this writing, it is believed that every person's fingerprint is unique to them. A concept that has never fully been even proven or disproven from my understanding. Let's take that concept to another level and think about how unique every spirit is. Made specially by God for a specific time in history and purpose both now and throughout eternity.

Now take these two unique and special spirits and combined them in a supernatural act called "sex" and mix them around over and over. Imagine the combination! When you mix a man and a man, you get a man. When you mix a woman and a woman you get a woman. But when you mix a Man and a Woman, what do you get then?

My best guess is you get the first "MAN" described in Genesis 1:26-27 (KJV) which says, ***"And God said, Let us make man in our image, after our likeness: and let them have dominion over the fish of the sea, and over the fowl of the*** *air, and over the cattle, and over all the earth, and over every creeping thing that creepeth upon the earth. So God created man in his own image, in the image of God created he him; male and female created he them."*

So, what is this original "MAN" that the Godhead created before putting him to sleep? I have no idea quite frankly. But I believe it's created again, every time a Male Spirit and a Female Spirit unite under God's purpose. This combined essence, or mixing, is even more special and unique than your fingerprint or your DNA, because it's unseen and only visible in God's Realm, the Spirit Realm.

I personally believe it frightens the devil and he hates it, which is why he wants to see men abuse and hurt their women instead of love and care for them. I think when a man abuses a woman, he's being used by the devil to try and destroy what God created in the Garden!

Don't let him use you to try and steal, kill and destroy the beautiful thing God created.

- **Mixing Red with Blue creates Purple.**
- **Mixing Flour with Water creates Dough.**
- **Mixing Soil with Seed creates a Tree.**

- **Mixing the Male Sperm with the Female Egg creates a Child.**
- **Mixing a Godly Man with a Godly Woman creates another form of GOD's Original Creation, made in His Image - ADAM.**

Question

If sex is more than just a physical act but a joining together with another person, how many people have you "joined" with that you should not have?

Now that you know that having sex is not just mixing bodies but mixing the essence of male and female, you will be more careful not to just jump in the bed with just anyone, right?

THE SKILLFUL FARMER

"Whatever you give a woman, she will make greater. If you give her sperm, she'll give you a baby. If you give her a house, she'll give you a home. If you give her groceries, she'll give you a meal. If you give her a smile, she'll give you her heart. She multiplies and enlarges what is given to her." ~William Golding

One of the most important things I want every guy who reads any of our content or engages with the CENTRY Brand in any way, to understand is this, I believe that a man that loves God is created, anointed and equipped by Him to love and to honor a woman. He also has the privilege to receive back from a woman whatever he has sown into her. What he doesn't want back from her, he shouldn't give out to her. It's as simple as that. However, it's a concept that many guys don't seem to understand, don't believe or just don't want to accept.

I want to help change that. So, let's talk about how a man can become a Skillful Farmer.

<u>STAGE 1</u>: <u>Understand the Process</u>

As we discuss how to be a skillful farmer, let's understand what it means to be a farmer. When a man understands how to be a farmer, he knows how to receive from the soil that he is working with. If you want to be a skillful farmer when it comes to the heart of your woman you must first know how to sow into her.

Let's talk about it.

<u>She Returns What's Given</u>

As we begin this topic let's start with a very simple, but I think a very powerful statement which is, "Only Sow into Her, What You Want to Grow and Come back from Her!"

If you can imagine a woman as an incubator, you will understand that she will return to you what you give to her. For example, as we have discussed already if you give a woman sperm she receives that sperm, it incubates and grows within her and she returns a child. So, whatever you give her she will return back to you in greater form and in greater measure.

So, with that said, don't do, don't say, don't treat and don't expect anything from her that you have not first given her and that you don't want to receive back from her. If you were a farmer and wanted to grow an apple tree, it would be unwise to plant corn seed. If you want to receive apples, you must plant apple seeds.

If you want to receive love, honor and respect from your woman, you must first plant the seeds of love, honor and respect into her. Don't plant the seeds of disrespect and dishonor into her and expect to receive love and honor back. That's just stupid! So, if you are doing that, you're an idiot!

Now that I've got that off my chest, let's move on.

Do You Have Access?

How silly do you think it would be for a farmer to try and sow seed into farmland that he doesn't own or have access to? What if a farmer walked up to a random gate, just through seeds over the fence and then expected ownership of any harvest that may come from it? Sounds silly right? Well, the same is true when a man causes the ground of his woman to close up through hurt, abuse, infidelity, disrespect, etc. and then expects her to respond to him with love and affection. If you lose access to her heart, no good seed is going to grow.

If you want your woman to bring forth seeds that you sow, she must allow you to sow into her. You will never receive a baby from a woman you have not had sex with or has not received your sperm in some manner. In the same way if you wanna harvest love and affection from your woman make sure her heart or her ground is open to you.

If you have closed her ground or her heart through your hurt or disrespect, it's important to first open her heart back up to you by asking for forgiveness, by rebuilding her trust or by doing whatever is necessary to restore her heart so that you can sow again. You will never receive a harvest from ground you have no access to.

STAGE 2: Prepare The Ground

Now that you have access to the ground, we need to test what type of ground it is. Let's be honest about the world that we live in. There is a lot of disrespect on both sides of the relationship fence when it comes to how men treat women and how women treat men.

I personally believe because of the amount of disrespect and dishonor that women have received from men, there is a large pushback from women on their viewpoint and their treatment of men. So, when it comes to the woman that you love, what type of ground does she have?

It's important to understand that, so that you know how to properly sow your seed into her. So, let's discuss the ground of your woman and how to prepare it to receive your seeds of love.

Test Her Soil

Keeping in mind that every woman is different as we've already stated, before you can properly sow seeds into her, you'll need to know what type of ground she has. Is she honorable towards men, or has she been constantly hurt and let down by them? Has she been raised with a loving father in her home, or does she even know who her father is? Have the men that have come before her treated her with love and honor or is she one of those one in three women that have been abused or mistreated by a man and is she's still harboring that pain in her heart?

These are important questions to understand and to ask not to disqualify her as your potential wife or someone that deserves your love, but to understand where she has come from and what you need to do to properly show her how much you love her and how much of God's love is available for her through you.

So, you're going to need to test the soil. Don't put your woman in a broad generalized category that says all women are crazy or all women are emotional. That's a childish, immature and unfair conclusion for any man of God to come to.

You must first with God's help, learn how to sincerely love, pray for and understand the type of woman you have through conversation, patience and understanding. By doing this, you can learn how to understand what type of soil God has given you, in the heart, the body and the spirit of the woman in your life.

She Returns Her Hurts

Ok, so if we understand that a woman returns what she is given, then if a woman is hurt, she will return hurts. If a woman is hurt by a man, she will return to a man attitudes, words and thoughts that express that hurt.

Now, let's be clear, some of the hurts she returns to you might not be yours. You may not be the actual source of some of the pain that comes forth from her heart. This is part of the process of properly selecting a woman that you can be in a fruitful relationship with where you but submit to each other, and become one in mind, body and soul. However, if she has been hurt by previous relationships, that she has yet to heal from, it may be difficult to sow into her ground and receive a good harvest because of what she has experienced in the past.

True story...one day I bought my girlfriend a single red rose. We were going out that evening so, I brought it in and laid it on the counter in front of her as she was doing her hair. She looked down at the rose and said, without missing a beat, "What's that for?" I could tell by her tone that she didn't receive the rose in the heart of appreciation and affection that I gave it to her in. So, without a word, I left the rose on the counter, turned around and left the room. It wasn't until my response didn't match her attitude, that she realized she was giving me something I didn't deserve.

So, in the same way, as men that want to love our women and wives as Christ loved the church, there may be times and situations that we might experience "mistreatment" or "dishonor" from our women that we have not sown for and don't deserve. It's at those times we have an opportunity to love them, as Christ loves us.

Meaning with God's help, we have an opportunity to love them beyond how they love us. To do for them at times beyond what they may have done for us. To respond to them at times beyond how they may have responded to us. To forgive them at times for treating us in ways that another man may actually deserve.

By understanding that your woman will return to you the hurts and disappointments that are in her, it helps equip you to help heal those hurts. Even if those hurts were caused by some immature and destructive guy she experienced before you came along. Or quite frankly, it could be hurts you caused her before you learned to love her properly and examine your treatment of her.

Either way, you can help your woman heal, by the love and the grace of God made available to you by our Lord and Savior Jesus Christ.

STAGE 3: Sow Proper Seeds

We've talked about it before, so we'll talk about it again, don't sow seeds that you don't want to receive. If you want to receive apples don't sow banana seeds. It's not rocket science, but it seems to be "uncommon" common sense for some guys. If you as a guy want to receive love, honor and respect from your woman, you must first sow kindness, love and honor into your woman. I just don't understand how some guys can abuse, mistreat and hurt women and then complain about how they respond as a result!

That's crazy right?! Or is it just me?

The Best Seed

As Christian men, there is one very simple and powerful seed that each of us should always be sowing, and that's the seed of love. Love will always harvest because it's the first and greatest seed that there is and that there will ever be.

1 John 4:7-8 (ESV) says, "***Beloved, let us love one another, for love is from God, and whoever loves has been born of God and knows God. Anyone who does not love does not know God, because God is love.***"

Now I'd like to take that verse a little deeper than just the surface interpretation. The verse says, God IS Love. Not that God HAS Love, or that God

133

<u>GIVES</u> Love, both of which are true. But this particular verse says, God <u>IS</u> Love. So, wherever you see LOVE, you see God. But before we go any further, let's discuss the several ways that the word "love" is interpreted in the Bible from the Hebrew or Greek language into English. This translation often causes us to miss the original purpose and meaning behind the word "love".

The Bible interprets the word Love as:
    #1 - Eros: Sensual or Romantic Love
    #2 - Storge: Family or Parental Love
    #3 - Philia: Brotherly or Friendship Love
    #4 - Agape: God's Eternal Unconditional Love

Each one of these forms of love expresses God so every time you express one of these forms of love you are expressing God because again God is love.

<u>"Eros (*AIR-ohs*) is the Greek term used for sensual or romantic love."</u> Eros Love is an expression of God because it helps men and women connect through affection and sexual intercourse while also creating lasting legacy of their connection when children are born to them as a result of their love and affection.

"**Storge** (*STOR-jay*) is the Greek term used to describe the bond between parents, children, brothers, sisters and family members.**" Storge Love is an expression of God because family is important to God. God is a God of family and He loves His own Heavenly Family, or the Trinity relationship, that He has with the Son and Spirit, along with all of the Angels and Creations we have yet to see or understand that keep Him company in Heaven. All of this expresses His love for family and companionship.

"**Philia** (*FILL-ee-uh*) is the Greek term that describes the powerful emotional bond seen in deep friendships.**" Philia Love is an expression of God because man, woman and friends develop bonds that helped them stand together in good and bad times. One of the strongest friendships I have was developed while growing up in Philadelphia. It was when my friend Mike stood next to me during a standoff with a group of bullies when other guys left us because we were outnumbered and possibly about to get a "Classic Philly Beat Down"! But because Mike didn't leave me, and I didn't leave him, we have developed a brotherly love that will last forever.

"**Agape (*Uh-GAH-pay*) is the Greek term used to try and describe the supernatural unconditional, immeasurable and never-ending love that God has for mankind.**" Agape Love is what each of us have an opportunity to experience from God both corporately and as individuals as we accept and believe in the finished works and sacrifice of Jesus Christ. Agape Love is what God has for everyone on the planet whether they receive Him, believe in Him, accept Him or reject Him. God's Agape love will never fail no matter how much the enemy wants to convince people that there is no God or try and get us to reject Him or the sacrifice that His Son did for us.

So, the best type of seed to sow is the seed of love into your woman, into your children and into others. When you sow the seed of love it will return to you even if it needs to return through another source because the person that you sowed the original seed of love into doesn't sow it back. It will come back to you, even if the person you gave it to doesn't return it to you.

Galatians 6:7-8 (NKJV) says, "***Do not be deceived, God is not mocked; for whatever a man sows, that he will also reap. For he who sows to his flesh will*** *of the flesh reap corruption, but he who sows to the Spirit will of the Spirit reap everlasting life."*

God's Word didn't say "where" your seed would come from, but that it would come. So, make sure to sow the best seed and that best seed is the seed of love. And every time you sow it, God is there because that act of Love is God.

Cultivate Her Ground

So, if you want to be a skillful farmer you must always be willing to cultivate, or care for, the ground that you have sown your seed into. This way you can expect to receive the very best harvest possible.

So be patient with your woman and her ground. Take the time to cultivate her ground as a skillful farmer with love, kindness, understanding and consistency knowing and believing that when you do receive your harvest, it will be something that's above and beyond all you can ask or think because you took the time to cultivate the ground.

STAGE 4: Expect a Harvest

One of the things that's important to understand and to believe is that a harvest will come from the good things that you sow, or the good things that you do. I've already shared the scripture, so I won't share it again, but remember, what you sow you'll receive. With that said, it's important to trust the process that God has put in place and to ignore some of the beliefs and negativity that comes from the world that agrees with and advances the mistreatment of the women and the children that we love.

So, expect a harvest when you sow good. If you expect a harvest from what you sow, then you'll make certain that what you sow is good.

Keep Her Ground Open

If the ground of her heart isn't fertile no seed will grow because infertile ground doesn't produce a harvest. With that said it's important to keep the ground of your woman's heart open to you. You do this by being mindful of the words you speak, the things you do, and being quick to repent and to adjust before her ground hardens towards you.

If you want to make sure that her ground stays open it's vital that you judge the words you speak, and the actions that you take, to make sure they are done from a heart of love and kindness. You still may mess up from time to time, but if your heart and your intention is to love her, to help her, to build her and to increase your relationship with her, it'll be easier to correct a minor mistake when you're headed in the right direction.

For example, if you do or say something that's totally based in selfishness and is only meant to help you and to get from her what you want, once that selfish act fails, it will be hard to win back her heart without completely admitting to your selfishness and on purpose doing something that's opposite of selfishness to show her that you love and care for her.

On the other hand, if your intention is to love and honor her and you mess up, or your actions are misunderstood, it'll be easier to help her see and understand what your true motive was, despite the misunderstanding because your intentions were pure.

So, every act you take will either keep the ground of your woman's heart open to you or move you towards causing her ground to harden and close up to you.

<u>Be Sure She's Comfortable</u>

A perfect way to make sure that her ground stays open is to make sure that she's comfortable with you and your relationship with her. You do this by being attentive, by spending time, by learning her love language and operating in that language. One of the things I like to tell guys is a very simple truth, "Just do whatever she tells you to do."

It's not rocket science and many of the things that our women need are not automatic and sometimes don't make sense to us as men. And sometimes we will miss it and not understand, but at least listen to what she says, and do your best to give her exactly what she asked for. So, if she says, "I need you to sit and listen to me." She's made it easy for you! Just sit your butt down and listen!

Sometimes we make it harder for ourselves as men when we try to figure everything out. Or we place our manly perspective on women, and than wonder why things aren't working out right! Not to mention, depending on who taught us that manly perspective, it could be completely wrong, twisted and causing more damage to our relationships than we can see.

So, make her comfortable by all means necessary. Keep her heart and ground open to you and the seed that you sow as a son of God.

STAGE 5: Repeat The Process

So, after you've learned what to sow, and how to sow, it should be easy to just repeat the process. Unfortunately, some guys start out great during the dating phase, then suddenly switch from that "Loving Man", that was sent from above, to some "Selfish Jerk", that crawled up from below. Don't be that dude that starts out good and drops the ball halfway through the game. Continue in your walk of love and repeat the process of love over and over and receive a heavenly reward for doing so.

So, let's talk about a few ways to do that.

Make Her Feel Beautiful

One thing that's important to keep in mind is that women think a lot more than men do. A study, published in the Journal of Alzheimer's Disease, concluded that, a woman's brain is significantly more active in several areas than a man's, especially in the prefrontal cortex which involves the focus, impulse control, and emotional areas of the brain responsible for mood and anxiety. However, the visual and coordination centers of the brain were more active in men. [12]

I share this to express how much more women are more likely to think about things than men are. So do not put ideas into the mind of your woman that make her feel as if she's not important or beautiful to you. Don't ever make her feel unwanted or compare her to another woman. Even if she has gained some extra weight here or there it does not change the fact that she may be the mother of your child or the woman that has been there for you faithfully over the years, during the good and the bad times.

If you really love her, then her body is your body. 1 Corinthians 7:4 NIV says, ***"The wife does not have authority over her own body but yields it to her husband. In the same way, the husband does not have authority over his own body but yields it to his wife."***

So, if "your body", that your woman is carrying, needs a little extra love to lose a couple of extra pounds, you love "your body" and take it to the gym with you. And you and "your body" spend some time on the treadmill together! Her body is "your body" and as a Son of God, you're required to love her always inside and out.

Avoid Seeds Of Doubt

In every situation we have an opportunity to believe the best or to believe the worst. When we aren't open with the people around us about what we're thinking, or how we're feeling, our silence can open the door for the other person to fill in the empty space of whatever it is that we're not saying, with whatever comes to their mind. Unfortunately, most of the time when people are left to come up with their own conclusions, they often think the worse. It's part of human nature.

So don't allow the seeds of doubt to drop into the heart of your woman because you keep things inside or you're not open with her. Always strive to keep her heart secure in the love you have for her and in her position in your life. Do not allow seeds of doubt to drop in her heart because you are gone for long hours and don't explain where you were or why you didn't answer the phone even if you weren't doing anything wrong.

And if you are trying to fix something that you may have broken, always be willing to uproot the doubt that's in her heart because of what you've done or the trust you've broken. Be man enough, and strong enough, to repair the damage and rebuild the wall that you, by your own actions, may have destroyed.

Even if she mentions the beauty or the shape of another woman, I strongly recommend that you do not entertain that conversation with her, and refocus the conversation back to how beautiful she is to you. It could be just me, but I don't wanna hear my woman talk about how fine another man is, I don't want those seeds of competition in my heart when it comes to my woman.

So, I make certain not to plant the seeds of doubt in her heart about some other woman. Some people may say, "Eric, you need to be more secure in who you are." But I lean on a very powerful saying I heard, and I believe with my whole heart which is this, *"A man doesn't stay with a woman because of how he feels about her; he stays with her because of how he feels about himself, when he's with her."*

So, if you're with someone that makes you feel like you don't measure up in comparison to someone else, it's better to go and find someone else that will love you completely for who you are without comparisons. Don't allow someone to put seeds of doubt within you because of who you are or who you're not. Don't allow the seeds of doubt to interrupt the peace and tranquility of your home and your relationship.

God made you perfect the way you are. So, if someone doesn't see that, you need to make both a simple and maybe difficult decision, move on and let God lead you to someone that will love and accept you for the awesome way He made you.

Adjust And Repeat

Finally, as we discuss the importance of being a skillful farmer, it's important to pay attention to the process. We've mentioned some vital keys here, but these keys will need to be adjusted based on you, your situation, the woman in your life, your history, your upbringing and the specific qualities that make you unique.

So, when it comes to learning how to sow properly into the ground, heart and spirit of your woman, you're going to have to examine, adjust, learn and grow as you continue to cultivate the relationship you have with her. Once you've figured out what works, repeat the process so that you'll continue to receive a good harvest from her from generation to generation.

Question

If you really understand that you receive back from your woman what you've given to her, are there any areas where you know she's returning to you the negative things that you've given to her?

If so, how do you plan to uproot those negative seeds and plant positive ones?

WHY HONOR HER?

"Love is an act of endless forgiveness, a tender look which becomes a habit." ~Peter Ustinov

Sometimes men look for the easy way out. It's easy to do what takes the least amount of work or thinking. However, despite all of the things that make a woman special and amazing to look at and spend time with, one of the most important reasons to honor her is by choice.

You honor her because she's special. You honor her because she's unique. You honor her because she's made to be cherished and held, not abused or hurt. Have you ever seen how people treat fine china, or a very valuable vase? They're purposely put in a special place of care and safety because they're precious and special.

They sit on pedestals and are guarded in cabinets because the people that own them choose to appreciate their value. They understand how precious these pieces really are. The reason why women have not experienced the honor they deserve from men is because we men have yet to truly understand how special women really are.

147

It's only when a person doesn't know the value of fine china or a special vase, that they place it just anywhere in the house where it can be damaged and broken.

A guy that doesn't care about the words he uses with his woman, that's not mindful of the strength he uses when handling her and doesn't care about her feelings, does so because he just doesn't know what he has, or how valuable a woman is. He's like a little boy playing baseball in the China shop. He's just not mature enough to respect and value what's around him.

The word "honor" is described as, *"high respect, as in worth, merit, or rank: to hold in honor or high respect; revere: to treat with honor. to confer honor or distinction upon."* By these descriptions you will see that honor is a choice and a decision. It's a quality stance and perspective, made by a quality person. Only males of honor have the ability to show honor. And if you're not a male of honor you can become one today by deciding to give honor.

Men, we ask that you consider the way a woman is made; smaller in strength and stature so protect her because of it. Consider how a woman sometimes has fragile feelings and emotions, so be concerned about them because of it.

Consider a woman's body. How it's wonderfully made shapely, gentle and soft. So don't just damage, hurt and abuse it. Appreciate her because of it. We ask that you consider who and what the special woman in your life means to you, what your life would be without her and honor her by choice because of it.

Question

Can you list three reasons why you as a man, should always love and honor women?

**Love all, trust a few.
Do wrong to none.**

~ William Shakespeare

PART 5:
EXPRESSION

"In the same way, let your light shine before others, so that they may see your good works and give glory to your Father who is in heaven." ~Matthew 5:16 ESV

What you think, what you believe and what you've been taught is what you express to the world around you. If you really want to be a Son of God that shows the world, and the women you come in contact with, how much God loves them, it's important to make sure that your thoughts and perspectives about yourself and others are in line with the love of God.

Every Christian man should desire to express what Christ has done for him and I believe the strongest expression of this begins at home behind closed doors with the woman that sees him at his most natural, at his most true and his most sincere self without blinders or false pretense.

This is a man that God wants to see Jesus Christ manifesting in his life.

MATURE MINDSETS

"Brothers, do not be children in your thinking. Be infants in evil, but in your thinking be mature."
~1 Corinthians 14:20 ESV

Some of the ways guys think and act are quite frankly childish and immature. In many instances, a guy's mindset isn't designed to help people, further relationships or enhance families. Many of the ways that guys think and act, quite frankly, are self centered and destroy the very foundation of our families and community.

As we continue to pursue being the type of men that express the love of God it's important that we let go of immature mindsets and replace them with mature and godly ones.

Love Takes Strength

Our current society has confused what true strength is. True strength is not measured in your physical height or the items you possess. True strength is measured in your ability as a Christian man and son of God to look like your Heavenly Father, follow your Heavenly Father's instructions and express the love of your Heavenly Father to those that you come in contact with. This strength has nothing to do with how they treat you or how they view you. The world around us hated Jesus when he walked the earth, and he told us they will hate us as well. True strength of a man of God is seen in the love he's able to show when he's tired; in the love he's able to show when he feels unwanted; and in the love he's able to show to others when he doesn't feel loved in return. True love is seen in a Man of God because the love he shows wasn't given to him by the World, it was given to him by God. So, the world can't take from him what the world didn't give him.

Let God's Love flow through you, and His Love will be your strength.

Every Woman IS NOT A Conquest

Speaking again to the mindset of childish men that pursue sex as a way of life, this is not the mindset of a man that wants to be pleasing in the eyes of God. In the eyes of God, every woman is his daughter, and He loves and cares for her, even if she doesn't love or care for Him in return. God doesn't want His Sons to view every attractive, sexy or even available woman he meets, as a sexual conquest to be used for his pleasure.

As a son of God, it's vital to understand that you will meet women that are attractive, that are lovely and that appeal to you physically but that doesn't make them an automatic sexual conquest. Some of these women you may need to encourage. Some may need you as a brother. And some may simply need to experience the kindness from you as a man that wants nothing from them in return because that may be all they've ever experienced. Some of these women will need to feel the love of God flowing through your life and God may have ordered your steps to come in contact with them for that very purpose.

So once again, every woman is not a conquest. There may be some women that you just need to love, honor and support for a short season of her life. Be strong enough to have a standard that says I will honor and cherish every woman I come in contact with because that is what will please my Heavenly Father.

Real Men Don't Hit Women

This is one of my biggest hurts when it comes to what men do and how men treat women. A real man should never justify physically abusing or hitting a woman no matter what she does. Under normal circumstances, a woman is not created to stand physically equal to a man. She doesn't have the physical strength in her shoulders. She doesn't have the same coordination with her fist or arms. God did that on purpose. She wasn't created to easily defend herself against a man. So, when a man hits and abuses a woman, it is not a fair fight from the beginning and only cowards enter a fight they know they will probably win. Most guys that hit women wouldn't do so, if her big brother or her father were standing there. That would change the game completely!

A real man wouldn't fight someone he knew he could easily beat. A real man wouldn't kick a puppy, or smack a child, that couldn't fight back and defend themselves because that's not what real men do. So, if you're a real man, make a conscious decision to never abuse someone who cannot defend themselves from you! That's not what real men do! And every woman and child have a Real God that'll defend and protect them! It's just a matter of time. Don't put yourself on the wrong side of their vengeful Father and God.

Stop Whining! God Did It!

Women are not made the same way that men are. I personally believe that is one of the reasons why a family needs a man and a woman to properly raise a child, because the perspectives, thoughts and actions of a man are different from those of a woman.

I believe a child needs to experience the strength of a father, along with the kindness of a mother. And the two need to interchange those roles at times to raise a well-rounded child. Of course, there are exceptions to this rule and single parents do awesome jobs! It just would be easier on them, I believe with help. But regardless, I don't believe men should complain about the differences between men and women because when you do, you're actually complaining about what God did and how He did it.

Instead of complaining about what God did, seek Him for help to understand the woman in your life, the women that you come in contact with, and the role that you are called to play as a Man of God when it comes to interacting with the daughters of the Most High. Don't whine about women.

Make a conscious decision to love them despite what you do and don't understand, and allow God to bring revelation and understanding on how to better love and honor the Daughters of the King that you encounter in life.

When You Don't Know, Ask

There's a very simple concept that I think a lot of guys just need to understand, and that is this, "You don't understand everything. Stop acting like you do!" When it comes to what women really need and really want, many times we don't know what they're thinking and we just don't know what they need. Fortunately, there's a simple and efficient way to figure it out; Ask. Ask her what she wants. Ask her what she's thinking. Ask her how she's feeling. And then just give her what she's asked for and you're good. BAMM!

Sounds simple, doesn't it? Then why don't more guys do it? What rule book are we guys reading that tells us exactly what to do for a woman created by God to give birth to kids, that develop both mentally and physically faster than us and that are meant to help and support us, as we help and support them? If anyone has an extra copy of this very important manual, please forward me a copy and I'll pay for the postage!

If we as men take the time to ask, we'll see that our women are very vocal about what they want and what they need. And sometimes if they don't know what to say, just having a man that cares enough to ask about their needs and desires may be enough to make them feel happy and secure.

So, what you don't know be man enough to ask.

Help Repair The Damage

There's a lot of selfishness in our society. We've discussed this and we will continue to see this I believe until Jesus comes back. However, one of the greatest things that I believe we will receive a reward for, is being a man that shows God's Light in this dark world. Matthew 5:16 (KJV) says, *"__Let your light so shine before men, that they may see your good works, and glorify your Father which is in heaven.__"*

The darkness in the world does not surprise God. He's not shocked at the destruction, the abuse, the perversion, and the evil that's in the world today. What if He's allowed the darkness to grow so that His sons and daughters can be the lights they've been called to be?

Think about this, the light from a candle burns at the same intensity both at nighttime and during the day. However, it's clearly seen and seems to burn brighter at night, not because it's intensity has changed, but because it's surrounded by

158

darkness. You are called to be a light and sometimes the Creator of the Light may allow you to be in the middle of darkness, just so that His Light in you, can shine brightly.

As a man of God, you have an opportunity to help repair the damage that has been done by selfish and evil men. There's many women and children that have been mistreated that may be healed by God's Grace flowing through your life. You'll never know what hurts or pains that He may want to use you to heal.

Like Your Mom, Wife & Daughter

When it comes to how you treat women that you come in contact with, keep in mind how you want your own mother, your wife, and your daughter to be treated by other men. If you want other men to love and respect your mother, your wife and your daughter when you're not around, make sure that you are honorable, respectful, kind and thoughtful to every woman you come in contact with. These women are the mothers, sisters and daughters of other men, so treat them the way you want your own women to be treated.

By doing so, you're on purpose sowing the seeds of love and honor for women in other guys lives, that you want to return on the women in your life. Make sure that your words, your thoughts and your actions are honorable towards other women, so that you've sown for those same types of words of love and acts of honor to be done for the important women in your life.

Treat every woman you come in contact with like you want your mom, your daughter, and your wife to be treated.

Question

There's always someone watching you. So, are you willing to be the type of man that helps other guys to love and honor the women in their lives because they see how you love and honor the women in your life?

GOD'S KIND OF LOVE

"Love is patient, love is kind. It does not envy, it does not boast, it is not proud. It does not dishonor others, it is not self-seeking, it is not easily angered, it keeps no record of wrongs. Love does not delight in evil but rejoices with the truth. It always protects, always trusts, always hopes, always perseveres. Love never fails. But where there are prophecies, they will cease; where there are tongues, they will be stilled; where there is knowledge, it will pass away. For we know in part and we prophesy in part, but when completeness comes, what is in part disappears. When I was a child, I talked like a child, I thought like a child, I reasoned like a child. When I became a man, I put the ways of childhood behind me. For now we see only a reflection as in a mirror; then we shall see face to face. Now I know in part; then I shall know fully, even as I am fully known. And now these three remain: faith, hope and love. But the greatest of these is love." ~1 Corinthians 13:4-13 NIV

As Sons of God, I don't think we can properly discuss how to love a Woman the way God wants her to be loved without discussing 1st Corinthians 13, often called the love chapter.

So, let's discuss what it says about love verse by verse.

161

Love Is Patient

Patience is one of the quickest and easiest ways to express love. When you rush a person to complete a task, or finish a thought, it expresses that you may not really be concerned about them or what they may be feeling, or expressing, at the moment, you just want them to get to the point. You rush people you are not concerned about. However, you are patient with people that are important, that you love and that you are mindful of. So, showing patience is a way of expressing love. So be patient with your woman. Be patient with your children. Be patient with the people that you say you care about because patience is an expression of love.

Love Is Kind

Being kind is an expression of love because it shows people that they're important to you. By being kind and gentle you show others that you're not purposely trying to upset or hurt them. It displays that they're important, that their thoughts are important and that their feelings are important because you're being kind. Kindness is also not an expression of weakness, even if some people may think it is. However, kindness is an expression of strength, especially when you know how to be kind to the people that really deserve it.

Love Is Not Envious

Enviousness is a way of trying to possess, or take what someone else has, while on the same hand, wanting to leave them with nothing. When you are envious, you not only want what the other person has, but you don't want them to have it, which is more selfish than anything. So, if you love a person, you're not envious of them. Even if you wish you had the same thing they have, because you love them, you want what they have, and you want them to have it too. You don't want them to lose, so you could have. That's not what love does.

Love Is Not Proud Or Boastful

When you're proud or boastful you're not expressing love because you by your words, thoughts or actions are trying to elevate, or exalt yourself above someone else. A person that's boastful, or prideful wants to stand above other people, which means they love themselves more than they love others and want to be seen as more important or successful than them. They want the other person to be beneath them, submissive to them or lesser than them, which is why they boast or are prideful because of what they have or what the other person doesn't have in their eyes. Being prideful or boastful is not an expression of love because it's a mindset that wants to elevate oneself, while on the same hand diminish someone else.

Love Does Not Dishonor

You can't give a person $5 out of your pocket, if there's not already $5 in your pocket, and you can't honor a person if you don't have honor within you. A person dishonors another person because they don't already possess the proper level of honor within them. And you'll only possess honor for someone when you respect and love them. When love or respect has stipulations, or conditions, dishonor will be the result. This is why racism, superiority, abuse, rape and molestation happen, because when differences in race, gender, age or desire come into play, selfish people choose themselves over others, which then justifies their acts or thoughts of dishonor. When you truly honor every person made in the image of God, there will be no justification for dishonor because you respect all people no matter what differences you have with them be it race, background, gender, age or beliefs.

Love Is Not Self-Seeking

When you're self seeking you're looking for ways to benefit and to elevate yourself. This again is not an expression of love because when you're self seeking you look for ways to benefit yourself, often at the expense of someone else. It's hard to be self seeking or to elevate yourself without on purpose diminishing the quality or the status of another person. This is why self seeking is not love because love always looks to benefit the other person and as you benefit them you will be benefited in return.

Love Is Not Easily Angered

Love isn't easily angered because true love is patient with people, even when it's disappointed or they don't agree. When you're easily angered, it's most likely because of some condition or expectation that you're holding someone too. So as soon as they stray from your expectation you become angered because of it. Being easily angered by people probably means that you're trying to control or manipulate them in some way, and you may use anger is a way to keep them in line. When you're easily angered at someone, they probably aren't in a proper place in your heart and your love and respect for them is probably very low or nonexistent. Once again when you love someone you are patient with them, which means you are not easily angered by them, and you are looking for ways to understand them and increase your relationship with them and anger gets in the way of that.

<u>Love Keeps No Record</u>

When you keep a record of the wrongs someone else has done, you're most likely keeping it so that you can use it against them either now, or in the future, to get something you want or to continue to make them pay for their past mistakes. But when you love someone, you don't purposely keep a record of what they've done wrong. Now there may need to be a period of restoration and healing from past hurts, but this period is used to help build and restore, not to maintain separation or to place blame. When you love someone, you're not on purpose looking for ways or things that you can hold against them. You're looking for ways to forgive them and to increase your relationship and your connection with them.

<u>Love Does Not Delight In Evil</u>

A person that's loving doesn't delight in the evil that separates friends and relationships. They aren't constantly gossiping, aren't constantly talking negatively or badmouthing others, and they don't find pleasure in the drama and hurt that separates friends and families. A person of love doesn't find delight when anyone experiences pain of any kind. But instead, they look and expect the best in others. Anyone that finds delight in evil is someone you should never spend time with because if you ever experience pain in your own life, they may act as if it hurts them in front of you, while in reality, they may not be upset at all.

Love Protects

What you love, you protect. A man should never use his strength against his woman, but only to help, to cover and to protect her. That's when a man's strength is truly needed and should be on display without question. When love is present in a man, acts of love should be seen from him. Those acts of love should be seen in his service, in his honor and in his protection that he shows for the people and the things he loves. His love should be positioned to protect them from any hurt and evil that tries to attack them whether it comes from others or even from within himself.

Love Always Trusts

When you love someone, you're always looking for ways to trust and believe in them. You work hard to think the best about them, and you quickly address concerns that may cause issues between you and them. When you love someone, you're quick to address thoughts, concerns and even people that may cause them hurt or that have the potential of damaging your trust in them. This could be something that the other person may take for granted at times, which may sometimes cause them to do things that damage your trust. Which then puts you in the position of trying to rebuild your trust in them again because of how much you love them.

Love Always Hopes

When you walk in love, you want the best for yourself and for the people around you. That's one reason why so many mothers, no matter what their sons do, always believe the best about them. It's their deep-rooted love that keeps them believing for them to do the right thing, even after multiple times of them falling short. Why? Because her motherly love always hopes for the best. Now if that's the case for a natural mother, how much more does our Heavenly Father's Love always hope for the best in us as his children because of the shed blood and sacrifice of our Lord and Savior Jesus Christ that equips us with everything we need to conquer and to win here on earth.

Love Always Perseveres

Thinking of Jesus and what He's done for us, He persevered through the shame, the pain, the suffering and the ridicule of the cross because of His love for us and because of the reward set before Him.

Hebrews 12:2 (NIV) says, "_...looking unto Jesus, the author and finisher of our faith, who for the joy that was set before Him endured the cross, despising the shame, and is set down at the right hand of the throne of God._"

If we want to display love like Jesus displayed for us, our love will need to persevere. It may be tested, it may get weak, and it may fall short at times, but with God's Grace, it'll last and hold strong. In the same way, our love for our women, our children and the people around us will last and persevere when it's not our love we are operating in, but we're allowing the love of our Lord and Savior Jesus Christ to flow through us and impact others and the world around us

Love Never Fails.

1 John 4:16 says, "_God is love, and all who live in love live in God, and God lives in them. God is love, and he who abides in love abides in God, and God in him. God is love, and he that dwelleth in love dwelleth in God, and God in him._"

Love never fails because God is Love. It doesn't say that God "HAS Love", but that God "IS Love" So whenever you see Love, you see God. God's Love can be seen in the kind words you speak to the strangers you pass in the street. God's Love can be seen in a young child hugging their parent, saying thank you. God's Love can be seen in the food on your table and the clothes on your back. Whenever you see and experience something in life that is good, it's actually an expression of God, because God is good.

Every time an act of kindness is done on the planet, it's because the presence and the Spirit of God is still here showing love to the good, and to the bad, to the righteous and to the unrighteous, because God is just that good. Love is from God and God never fails, so you are never failing when love is your motive, and your source. Do everything from a place of love and you'll never fail.

Question

Which of these areas of Love are the hardest for you to do? Do you have another guy, or mentor, that can help you when needed?

If you ever need counsel, we'd love to help. Contact us at: **ManhoodMentor.me**

5 WAYS TO HONOR HER

"To fear love is to fear life, and those who fear life are already three parts dead." ~Bertrand Russell

Ok, if you're still here, I believe that you're ready to truly start living in a way that honors women. We've spent the majority of our time together discussing what happens when you honor a woman and why you should. Now, let's talk about 5 ways you can truly give women the honor they need and deserve.

#1: <u>Refuse Destructive Change</u>

If you were trained to honor and respect women, then decide to be disrespectful or hurtful because of some selfish and childish guy talk, or because some stupid song called a woman a derogatory term like B@%CH or Hoe, you've allowed destructive change to turn you into a guy that hurts women instead of helps them. Don't let the people or conditions around you uproot the positive ways of acting and thinking that helped you become who you are. If you know it's wrong to hit a woman, and "YES, IT IS WRONG!", then you don't ever hit or abuse a woman – period. That standard doesn't change no matter what she does or what another selfish fool says is ok to do. What was wrong years ago is still wrong today, no matter how many people do it! It's important to avoid any destructive change that's meant to remove the quality standards that we lived by in the past. Don't allow destructive changes to take place in your thinking, your emotions or your standards that'll lead to a destructive outcome for you and the woman you love.

#2: <u>Reject Society Norms</u>

We learn our opinions and viewpoints from the environment we live in. Our parents, friends and neighborhood, along with the conversations we participate in and the music we listen to, all impact who we are. Some entertainment displays people with multiple sexual partners and no commitment while some music expresses a lifestyle of pursuing cash instead of purpose. It seems like the society we live in is purposely trying to replace the thoughts and standards that were good for us yesterday, with destructive habits and beliefs.

Sometimes the excuse I hear is, "People have changed.", which is not true. What has changed is our standards, our love and concern for each other and our acceptance of what's "wrong" based on how many people say it's "right". If you want to truly stand out as a strong quality man, and not just another selfish boy in our society, you must reject every thought and belief of our society that's meant to uproot the qualities and principles that made us strong as a people and individuals in the past. The choice is yours.

#3: <u>Be Different On Purpose</u>

If you actually apply the things we're talking about here, you'll be seen as different from the other childish and selfish guys in our society. So, if you're strong enough, accept it and be different on purpose. Stand out from the selfish jerks. Don't hit women. Don't pursue casual sex just for selfish pleasure and bragging rights. Be kind to a woman, just because she's a valuable woman, not because you need or want something from her. If you do just some of the things we're talking about, you'll stand out from the crowd. However, if you do them all and make them a way of life, you'll begin to change the way women are treated and how they feel about men. You'll have become different on purpose.

#4: <u>Give First; Receive Second</u>

Another thing that males need to be mindful of is the principle of giving first and then he's worthy to receive. I personally believe that a man should only require from a woman what he's already given her. If a man has not been affectionate or kind to a woman, he shouldn't expect affection or kindness. If a man hasn't been thoughtful, why should he be thought about? If a man has not rubbed her feet, why should she massage his back?! If a man is truly the leader, he should lead her by giving to her and then receiving from her.

Think about this, a woman is an incubator for everything that a man gives her. He gives her food; she makes a meal. He gives her a house; she makes a home. He gives her sperm; she gives him a baby. He gives her love and affection; she gives him submission and respect. The problem most guys have is that they expect to receive what they haven't given! Then they wonder what's wrong with her. It's because she's made to give back what you've already given her. If you haven't given her anything, she's got nothing to give back to you. It's like a guy walking up to an empty refrigerator and then complain about it being empty but he's put no food in it. How smart is that?!

#5: <u>Honor The Essence Of Women</u>

Men need to step back and see what beautiful creations women are and learn to honor the essence of what makes them great. Many of us men have become so selfish and self-centered in the misuse of women for our own selfish needs that we have become blind to the sheer beauty of women. Imagine an adult man walking through an art gallery of million-dollar paintings, taking the time to admire their value, beauty and variety. While behind him, a little boy ran through the same gallery pointing fingers, calling them ugly and laughing at the exact same paintings because he has no idea of their value.

As a whole, guys have been like little boys, unable to recognize the essence and beauty of what makes women special. Their shape, their hair, their smile, their walk, their voice and their gentleness are things to be honored and appreciated. If you can learn to honor the absolute and unquestionable essence and beauty of women, you'll be seen as a man worthy of honor and respect.

Question

Have you ever taken the time to just admire the differences between men and women to see the things that make women so special and unique?

If not, would you do me a favor and try?

Love isn't love until you give it away.

~ John H. MacDonald Jr.

30-DAY LOVE CHALLENGE

"Love isn't love until you give it away."
~ *John H. MacDonald Jr.*

I believe that males have the ability to show more of God's love than we think. God has given men the golden opportunity to be more like Him, if we would on purpose express unconditional love to others and especially our wives and women the same way He has expressed unconditional love to mankind. Guys, wanna test this theory? If so, try this **30-Day Unconditional Love Challenge**.

Ladies, please join us, especially if your man is!

Ok, Here It Is:

Get a piece of paper and write out how you feel about yourself as a man and how you feel about your woman / wife. Be honest, truthful, straight forward with yourself and don't let anyone see it. Place the piece of paper in a sealed envelope and put it away somewhere safe where even she can't find it. (You may want to give it to one of the guys to make sure it's nowhere in the house, especially if you wrote some things that may get you in trouble if she finds it.) Now, we challenge you for the next 30 days, despite how you feel or what she does, show her unconditional love on purpose. Don't ask her for anything in particular. Don't refuse anything she asks and don't make any "selfish or unnecessary requests" for 30 Days. Only *give and serve* her. If it's something that you can do for her, do it. If it's something you can do for yourself and not ask her, don't. You do it. You are not to ask or request anything from her for yourself personally, you are only to *give and serve* her kindness, service and affection for 30 Days.

Now, don't just give what's required like pleasant words. Every day it's important to find at least 3 things to do for her that she **_hasn't_** asked for. If she asks you to do something, still do it, but it doesn't count towards your daily goal of 3 things. It must be something that you do for her without it being requested by her. You are on purpose showing love without it being required. In addition to that, *every* and we do mean *every* act of kindness that comes into your mind, just do it. Now these don't have to be big things, actually small acts of service and kindness are the best. For example, get her a glass of water, bring her a flower, hold her hand, rub her feet, put gas in her car, iron her clothes. Just look around and you will always see something you can do for her, just make sure you do at least three every day.

There are no limits on how many things you *can* do, but there is a limit on how many things you *must* do. Again, you must do at least 3 a day. Make sure you mark the calendar, so that you know when your 30 days are up. Now, after the 30 Days are up, get another piece of paper and write down how you feel about yourself as a man, and how you feel about your woman / wife. Once you're done, open your first envelope and compare what you wrote on your first sheet with the second. So, what's the difference in how you felt 30 days ago compared to how you feel now? Do you feel different? If you did 3 Unconditional Acts of Love for her everyday, I'm sure you do.

Please share how you feel and download a chart to keep track with your 3 things at: CentryLeague.com/LoveChallenge

For those who are actually strong enough to take and complete this challenge, I truly believe that you'll begin to experience what it feels like to truly love unconditionally.

Question

Are you willing to take the 30-Day Unconditional Love Challenge with your wife, fiancé or special woman in your life? If so, please let us know!

Love is, above all else, the gift of oneself.

~ Jean Anouilh

JOIN THE CAUSE

"Love doesn't make the world go 'round. Love is what makes the ride worthwhile." ~Franklin P. Jones

At this point, I want to stress something very important. If we're ever to change our society, guys must learn to take responsibility for the respect and honor we show all women. Quite frankly, if you speak a kind word to a woman, it may be the only kind word she gets that day. If you compliment her outfit, without undressing her with your eyes, you may have been the only man that day, that appreciated her beauty without disrespecting her. If you open the door for her, you may have been the only gentlemen she has encountered in a long time, if ever. It's time that every quality male becomes more mindful of every woman he comes in contact with and use every opportunity he has to express love and honor to every woman that crosses his path.

Question

If every guy decided to purposely love and honor each and every woman he encounters, what do you think would happen to our communities and to the world?

We can only learn to love by loving.

~ Iris Murdoch

TAKE THE PLEDGE

I _____, Do Solemnly Pledge to Love, Honor and Respect Women. I Will Endeavor to Always Be a Gentleman. I Believe That Every Woman is a Gift from God. Despite How a Woman Treats Me, I will Speak Kindly to Her and Treat Her with Respect and Honor. I Understand That I Have No Idea What Type of Hurt A Woman May Have Experienced in Her Life from a Guy and How It May Have Impacted Her. So, Because I am a Strong Man of Honor, Respect and Love, I will Not Emotionally Abuse, Physically Abuse or Sexually Abuse a Woman. I will Protect Every Mother, Every Sister, Every Daughter and Every Wife from All Forms of Abuse to The Best of My Ability and I Will Be An Example to Guys on What it Means to Be a Man that Truly Loves Women by the Expression of Service, Honor, Protection, Respect, Consideration, Value and Appreciation I Show Them.

This, I do Pledge, on this Day of _____ in the year of Our Lord _____.

Download or forward the Pledge Online at:
CentryLeague.com/ThePledge

Real love is a permanently self-enlarging experience.

~ M. Scott Peck

CLOSING

"Love is a fruit in season at all times, and within reach of every hand." ~Mother Teresa

The way we, as a society, abuse and misuse women and children must stop! How much sense does it make for guys to abuse women when they are the source by which every guy was born? Absolutely None! The only one that would want this type of abuse and dishonor would have to have a plan to destroy the human race.

You can be a man that other men follow and admire. Help us rebuild the love and trust that our wives, our mothers, our sisters and our daughters deserve. We believe in you. Please believe in yourself. Join us in our mission to Serve, Honor and Protect as Servants, Soldiers & Heroes that are Fruitful and Multiply.

To Your Success...
Eric M. Watterson & The CENTRY League, LLC

If you enjoyed this book, please give it a
5 Star Review on Amazon.com.

Thanks so much and God Bless!

I don't think anyone can DO anything that would make him worthy of love. Love is a gift and cannot be earned. It can only be given.

~ Real Live Preacher

CLOSING PRAYER

"Heavenly Father, I as a man, thank you for the precious and special gift that You've provided us men, in women.

I admit that many times they're a mystery to me despite how much I'm drawn to their shape, their smell, their hair, their walk and all of the things that make them so attractive, so special, so captivating and so unique to me.

Father, please forgive me for every time I have mistreated a woman and used her for my own pleasure or satisfaction.

I ask You to help me to see women as a Gift from You and help me to honor them in a way that pleases You. Father, please show me how to love and honor my mother, sister, friend, girlfriend, fiancé, wife or wife to be with Your Love.

I ask and receive Your Grace to Love, Serve, Honor & Protect every one of Your daughters that I encounter. May my life be used from this point on to display only honor and value for every GIFT of HER, in Jesus Name I ask and pray, Amen."

BIBLIOGRAPHY

References Cited:

- [1] cdc.gov/violenceprevention/pdf/nisvs_report2010-a.pdf
- [2] bjs.gov/content/pub/pdf/ndv0312.pdf
- [3] cdc.gov/violenceprevention/pdf/nisvs_report2010-a.pdf)
- [4] nnedv.org/downloads/Census/DVCounts2013/DVCounts13_NatlSummary.pdf
- [5] cdc.gov/violenceprevention/pdf/nisvs_report2010-a.pdf
- [6] webmd.com/anxiety-panic/guide/self-injuring-hurting#091e9c5e800092de-1-3
- [7] livescience.com/45510-anno-domini.html
- [8] 1.grc.nasa.gov/beginners-guide-to-aeronautics/newtons-laws-of-motion/
- [9] ministry127.com/resources/illustration/father-s-day-card
- [10] Foubert, J. D., Brosi, M. W., & Bannon, R. S. (2011). Pornography viewing among fraternity men: Effects on bystander intervention, rape myth acceptance and behavioral intent to commit sexual assault.18(4), 212-231. doi:10.1080/10720162.2011.625552
- [11] Foubert, J. D., Brosi, M. W., & Bannon, R. S. (2011). Pornography viewing among fraternity men: Effects on bystander intervention, rape myth acceptance and behavioral intent to commit sexual assault.18(4), 212-231. doi:10.1080/10720162.2011.625552
- [12] weforum.org/agenda/2017/08/women-have-more-active-brains-than-men-according-to-science/

The Holy Bible:

- King James Version
- New International Version
- New Living Translation
- Amplified Version

Websites Used:

- The Quotations Page: (quotationspage.com)
- Dictionary.com: (dictionary.reference.com)
- WiseOldSayings.com: (wiseoldsayings.com)

FOLLOW US @

Facebook.com/iamcentry

Instagram.com/iamcentry/

YouTube.com/@centry

If you enjoyed this book, please give it a
5 Star Review on Amazon.com

Thanks so much and God Bless!

MORE CONTENT:

SERVE · HONOR · PROTECT

For more content and information concerning the CENTRY™ Brand, along with Additional Books, Courses, Content and Offers intended to Serve, Honor & Protect our wives, children, families, communities and the world.

For more information visit:
CENTRY.me or **CentryLeague.com**

The CENTRY™ League "**Choose Greatness Series & Program**" consists of our series of workbooks and online courses that we use to mentor and coach males in 7 Specific Areas that will inspire, assist and lead them to Choose Greatness in their lives.

For more information visit:
ChooseGreatness.me